W9-CDW-395

LIVING FAITH

"With the increasingly destructive manifestation of religious violence around the globe, this book presents powerful stories of 'visionary activists,' who, guided by their different faith traditions, inspired millions to pursue peace and justice.... In comparison to other sources on religion and peace, this book is rooted in a revolutionary social-justice analytical framework and successfully combines inspirational quotes from Muslim, Christian, and Buddhist leaders. This book is a must-read, especially for those who still have doubts about the relevancy of spirituality in the pursuit of justice and peace, and those who utilize religious identity as a dehumanizing tool."

—Mohammed Abu-Nimer—
American University's School of International Service,
Executive Director of the Salam Institute

"It is exciting to see the religious heart and soul of my father's work appreciated and espoused by Curtiss DeYoung's *Living Faith*."

—Ms. Malaak Shabazz—
Trustee of the Malcolm X & Dr. Betty Shabazz
Memorial & Education Center

"Religion is too often a divisive force in the world, abused in giving legitimacy to ideologies and practices that dehumanize others.... By telling the story of twentieth-century faith-activists, Curtiss DeYoung has provided a road map for all, irrespective of tradition, who recognize the deep connection between spirituality and the struggle for justice and peace. His passion for his subject is evident on every page, making his lively study a challenging document of faith and hope."

—John W. de Gruchy—
Professor of Christian Studies Emeritus,
University of Cape Town

LIVING FAITH
HOW FAITH INSPIRES SOCIAL JUSTICE

CURTISS PAUL DEYOUNG

Fortress Press   Minneapolis

LIVING FAITH
How Faith Inspires Social Justice

Copyright © 2007 Fortress Press, an imprint of Augsburg Fortress. All rights reserved. Except for brief quotations in critical articles or reviews, no part of this book may be reproduced in any manner without prior written permission from the publisher. Visit http://www.augsburgfortress.org/copyrights/contact.asp or write to Permissions, Augsburg Fortress, Box 1209, Minneapolis, MN 55440.

Cover images: Aung San Suu Kyi at a press conference in Yangon, February 25, 1999, © Reuters/Corbis; Malcolm X in Rochester, New York, February 16, 1965 © Michael Ochs Archives/Corbis; Dietrich Bonhoeffer, 1944 © Gütersloher Verlagshaus, Gütersloh, in der Verlagsgruppe Random House GmbH, München.
Cover design: Kevin van der Leek Design
Book design: Jill C. Lafferty

Library of Congress Cataloging-in-Publication Data
DeYoung, Curtiss Paul.
  Living faith : how faith inspires social justice / Curtiss Paul DeYoung.
    p. cm.
  Includes bibliographical references.
  ISBN-13: 978-0-8006-3841-2 (alk. paper)
  ISBN-10: 0-8006-3841-7 (alk. paper)
  1. Belief and doubt. 2. Faith. 3. Social justice—Religious aspects. 4. Social justice. I. Title.
  BD215.D45 2007
  201'.7—dc22
                      2006026167

The paper used in this publication meets the minimum requirements of American National Standard for Information Sciences—Permanence of Paper for Printed Library Materials, ANSI Z329.48-1984.

Manufactured in the U.S.A.

CONTENTS

1

MYSTIC-ACTIVISTS: AN INTRODUCTION

One evening near midnight, in the midst of the bus boycott in Montgomery, Alabama, the phone rang at the home of Martin Luther King Jr. The caller said, "Nigger, we are tired of you and your mess now. And if you aren't out of this town in three days, we're going to blow your brains out, and blow up your house." Shaken by the threat and the ugly voice, King sat down in his kitchen and poured himself some coffee. Sitting at the table he prayed, "Lord, I'm down here trying to do what's right. I think I'm right. I think the cause we represent is right. But Lord, I must confess that I'm weak now. I'm faltering. I'm losing my courage." King said he felt an inner voice say, "Martin Luther, stand up for righteousness. Stand up for justice. Stand up for truth. And lo I will be with you, even until the end of the world."[1]

King's kitchen experience implanted in the very depths of his soul a passion for social transformation. Martin Luther King Jr. was one of a number of leaders in the twentieth century whose ardent religious faith inspired their social activism. A nearly mystical awareness of God's presence "enabled him to make that contribution in the face of enormous and frightening opposition. And what that sense did for him personally, it also did for much of the movement as a whole."[2] Like King, many other social justice activists in the twentieth century embraced a faith that gave them courage and vision against great odds. And their personal faith emboldened the movements they led.

The twenty-first century inherits the spiritual devastation of the previous century. We live in a world shaken and dispirited by multiple traumas. The Holocaust in Nazi Germany and the U.S. dropping of nuclear bombs on Japan in the 1940s were turning points in a growing disillusionment with modern idealism. The assassinations of civil rights leaders in the 1960s led to the loss of hope among many in the United States. The Rwandan genocide of the 1990s exposed a religion not only incapable of reconciling ethnic tensions in society, but also culpable in horrific violence. The terrorist attacks of September 11, 2001, demoralized the United States and the international community as well—and revealed again religion's ability to tryst with fear and violence. These moments in history, along with many equally tragic incidents, shattered traditionally held assumptions and ideals. One survivor of Hiroshima thought to herself as the nuclear bomb dropped, "There is no God, no Buddha.... There is no God, no help."[3] What does this mean for today's emergent leaders and how they envision the possibility of reconciliation and social justice?

I revisit the hopeful vision and practices of twentieth-century faith-inspired social justice activists to discover inspiration for leaders in the twenty-first century, who will guide us in our search for a more just world. The evil in the world that killed Mohandas Gandhi, Dietrich Bonhoeffer, Malcolm X, Martin Luther King Jr., Oscar Romero, and others has extinguished the hopeful vision of many. Yet these martyred activists were willing to sacrifice their lives because they believed that it was possible to create a future that was more just and more reconciled. Some have seen the fruits of hopeful perseverance. Rigoberta Menchú has lived to see increased peace and justice in Guatemala, and she continues to strive for the fulfillment of her hopes. Nelson Mandela, Desmond Tutu, and Allan Boesak have lived to see a peaceful transition from a white supremacist government to one that seeks truth and reconciliation in a liberated South Africa. Others wait with a holy patience, such as Aung San Suu Kyi of Burma (Myanmar). Even while living under house arrest, imposed by Burma's current dictatorship, she still hopes that one day she will see freedom and democracy in her country. There are many more stories. Will there be similar stories to tell about leaders in the twenty-first century? Or will despondency and resignation prevail? Today, more than ever, we need leaders who choose to resist despair and embrace faith and hope.

The Evolution of My Interest in Faith and Activism

My interest in faith-inspired social justice activists began in 1970 when I was twelve years old. I, a white boy, resided in a suburb of Kalamazoo, Michigan. I lived a rather sheltered life common to many whites in the northern United States. Issues of social or racial justice rarely entered my world. Then, one evening in 1970, I watched a documentary called *King: A Filmed Record...Montgomery to Memphis.*[4] It was full of news footage and commentary on the Civil Rights Movement and the late Martin Luther King Jr. Before that night, I hadn't been aware of King or the Civil Rights Movement. That rapidly changed as I read every book I could find about King and this movement. I eagerly sought out recordings of his speeches. I wrote papers in my high school classes on King.

I attended Anderson College (now University) in Anderson, Indiana, in the late 1970s. I discovered that my campus pastor, James Earl Massey, had been a friend of Martin Luther King Jr. Through Massey, I discovered the writings of Howard Thurman, a mystic-theologian who had spiritually mentored many of the leaders in the Civil Rights Movement, including King. In my college classes, I began to learn about others from the Christian tradition who embraced reconciliation and social justice, including Dietrich Bonhoeffer and Jim Wallis. After graduation, I moved from the Midwest to New York City to work with homeless youth at Covenant House. I lived in a Roman Catholic Franciscan lay community where I learned about Saint Francis's passion for the poor. Also living in this community were friends of Dorothy Day, the founder of the Catholic Worker Movement who had died a year earlier. They told me about her life advocating for the poor and against war. They also shared with me the writings of Thomas Merton, a Catholic monk who bridged western and eastern mystical traditions, and introduced me in person to Father Daniel Berrigan, the peace activist.

In the early 1980s, I enrolled at the Howard University School of Divinity in Washington, D.C.—one of the nation's most respected African American institutions of higher education. The seminary lived and breathed liberation thought and action. Many on the faculty had participated in the Civil Rights Movement and had known Martin Luther King Jr. During my time at Howard University, one of King's closest associates, Bernard Lee, was also studying there—finally keeping his promise to King to finish his ministerial studies. I took a master's level course on the life and thought of Martin Luther King Jr. taught by Calvin S. Morris, a former member of King's staff at the Southern Christian Leadership Conference (SCLC). Howard Thurman had died two years before I arrived, but his thought permeated the school. In my coursework, I was introduced to black liberation theology and Latin American liberation theology. I even heard a lecture by Gustavo Gutiérrez—a founder of liberation theology. Desmond Tutu spoke in a chapel convocation. I also learned about the work of Malcolm X while at Howard University.

Since completing my divinity school studies in 1985, I have spent over twenty years seeking to better understand the essence of reconciliation and social justice. I have sought through building relationships, observing oppression and injustice first hand, experimenting with practical solutions, reading and researching widely, writing reflectively, and consistently stepping out of my comfort zone. This journey has taken me across the United States to small towns and big cities, as well as across the world to South Africa and Israel/Palestine. I have developed relationships with activists in places I have yet to visit. My journey is ongoing.

I conceived of this book sometime in the early 1990s because of a particular interest in and kindred spirit with Dietrich Bonhoeffer, Malcolm X, and Martin Luther King Jr. Since they had inspired my own life and work, I wanted to gain a deeper understanding of their vision and activism. Courses I took in feminist thought made me aware that a study of men trained in Western settings limited my own vision. So I began to research the lives and writings of Aung San Suu Kyi and Rigoberta Menchú. Suu Kyi and Menchú offered women's viewpoints, additional faith perspectives (Buddhist and indigenous), and non-Western lenses (Asia and Latin America).

As this book took shape, three representative leaders emerged: Dietrich Bonhoeffer, Malcolm X, and Aung San Suu Kyi. These three anchor this book. They offer a range of time periods, cultural settings, gender perspectives, and faith traditions. Dietrich Bonhoeffer was a Christian German white man who resisted the Nazi government during the 1930s and 1940s. Malcolm X was a Muslim African American man who struggled against racism in the 1950s and 1960s. Aung San Suu Kyi is a Buddhist Burmese woman who led the freedom movement in her country during the 1980s and 1990s. The two men's lives are entirely within the twentieth century. In the case of Suu Kyi, I focus primarily on her work in the twentieth century. While I chose these three as the central figures, I also incorporate the viewpoints and life experiences of other twentieth-century faith-inspired activists. These are from diverse cultural and religious settings throughout the world, including Martin Luther King Jr., Rigoberta Menchú, Nelson Mandela, Winona LaDuke, Oscar Romero, Fannie Lou Hamer, Elie Wiesel, Mohandas Gandhi, Dorothy Day, Desmond Tutu, Thich Nhat Hanh, Abraham Heschel, Allan Boesak, and the Dalai Lama.

My viewpoints and life experiences significantly influence the interpretation I offer of these leaders' lives. I do not aspire to present an unbiased stating of facts. I write with an agenda and a passion. I explore the essence of leaders who struggle for social justice with a religious faith guiding their efforts. My method is most like what sociologist Sara Lawrence-Lightfoot calls social science portraiture, which "is a method of qualitative research that blurs the boundaries of aesthetics and empiricism in an effort to capture the complexity, dynamics, and subtlety of human experience and organizational life.... Portraitists write to inform and inspire readers."[5]

An obvious difference between the way Lawrence-Lightfoot uses social science portraiture and the approach I use is the relationship with the individuals in the study. Her research is with living persons she interviews and observes. My research involves the words and life stories (as the subjects and multiple biographers relate it) of individuals who were unavailable for interviews due to death or inaccessibility. Two of the three leaders are dead, and the third, Aung San Suu Kyi, lives under house arrest in a totalitarian regime. Lawrence-

Lightfoot points out that "portraits are constructed, shaped, and drawn through the development of relationships."[6] Given the many years I have interacted with these texts and narratives, a relationship of sorts has developed with the persons. The impressions I have gained from the lives and works of social-justice activists date back to the early 1970s. I have studied Dietrich Bonhoeffer since the late 1970s, Malcolm X since the mid-1980s, and Aung San Suu Kyi since the early 1990s.

My own journey colors the way I see, interpret and present the journeys of others. Lawrence-Lightfoot suggests that "the portraitist inevitably renders a self-portrait that reveals her soul but she also produces a selfless, systematic examination of the actors' images, experiences, and perspectives. This balance—between documenting the authentic portrait of others and drawing one's self into the lines of the piece... is the difficult, complex, nuanced work of the portraitist."[7] Indeed, part of my soul is interwoven with the words and lives of these whose stories inspire and encourage me. My background—white, middle class, male, American—and my training in the Christian religious tradition affect my interpretation and conclusions. I have sought to write from an interfaith perspective, with a great respect for religious and cultural traditions other than my own. I hope I have learned from the insights of persons I have studied through the years.

Unique Kind of Activist

At first, I thought of these leaders as *visionary activists*.[8] I use the word *visionary* to mean one who is able to see clearly what causes injustice and to see how injustice gives birth to oppressive social conditions. A visionary is also able to see clearly what creates a just society (and believes in the possibility of achieving this). Robert Kennedy's famous words (paraphrasing George Bernard Shaw) capture how I apply *visionary* to these leaders, "Some [people] see things as they are, and say why; I dream of things that never were, and say why not?"[9] As visionaries, such leaders recognize injustice and are able to envision a just world. As activists, they design and implement ways of moving toward that just world. Visionary activists put flesh on their visions for a better world. They believe that vision and action go hand in hand. They follow the biblical declarations that without a vision the people perish (Prov 29:18); the just shall live by faith (Rom 1:17); and faith without action is dead (Jas 2:17).

Yet the term *visionary activist* does not fully capture the essence of this breed of leader. These leaders discover their activism through their religious faith. They discern and sustain their hope for the future through a spirit of mysticism. I borrow the term *mystic-activist* from Alton B. Pollard III to identify these leaders.[10] Pollard uses this term to describe Howard Thurman. He was a mystic in the traditional sense, pursuing the personal experience of the spiritual. But Thurman didn't remain hidden it that inward journey. He also sought to engage with society, particularly regarding racism, and he reached out to activists as a spiritual mentor. Catholic monk Thomas Merton is another example of a contemplative who spoke to social justice issues. For both, mysticism was a point of departure.

Most religious traditions identify certain people as mystics or contemplatives. These individuals pursue a "direct experience of ultimate reality"[11] or "the experience of some form of union with God."[12] Mysticism cannot be defined completely because it speaks of the mystery of religious faith. Mystical encounters defy "conceptualization and verbalization."[13] If the experience can be described definitively, then it is not mysticism. Mystics talk of visions and ecstasy, describing their peak experiences using "colorful language and poetry to convey the gist of it."[14] According to Thomas Merton, the contemplative seeks to "recover the light and the capacity to understand what is beyond words and beyond explanations because it is too close to be explained: it is the intimate union in the depths of your own heart, of God's spirit and your own secret inmost self."[15]

I expand Pollard's notion of mystic-activism. Most faith-inspired activists are not mystics or contemplatives in the purest traditional sense. I use *mystic-activist* to speak also of leaders whose activism consumes them yet is deeply rooted in their faith and in the mystery of the divine. Their activism compels them to reach passionately inward toward the divine for sustenance, wisdom, perseverance, and belonging. Their outward activism needs inward mysticism.

I use Pollard's term, *mystic-activist,* to describe the spiritual quality of the activism of such leaders. Descriptors like *religious, faith-based,* and *spiritual* are often imprecise or even carry negative connotations for some. I also use *mystic* to distinguish the faith experience I discovered in the lives of these activist movement leaders. Mystics often are thought of as people who seem strange, otherworldly, or superstitious. This is not a helpful view of mystics. I use *mysticism* to speak of a faith experienced through a direct relationship with the divine in contrast to a religion mediated through rituals or rules. The activists in this study testify of a vibrant, alive, and engaged faith.

In their book *Oscar Romero: Reflections of His Life and Writings,* authors Marie Dennis, Renny Golden, and Scott Wright note that activists or prophets "who are caught in the fire of history and nudged by the great maw of justice rarely court the inner realms of mysticism.... Conversely, mystics are said to avoid the marketplace and to seek the gates of silence which swing open to the rapture of God." This is a false dichotomy. Dennis, Golden, and Wright conclude, "Few prophets could endure the scandal and scourge they evoke without an inner life of fathomless depth and intensity. And few who climb the mystical mountain of Carmel reach the great heights of Mystery without walking back down to embrace the ragtag people pushing history toward blessing or curse."[16]

Outline of the Book

I have discovered a number of shared themes—or ways of being—emerging from the lives of faith-inspired social-justice activists. I examine and focus upon four themes that appear, to varying degrees, in each of their lives: (1) their religious faith motivates them; (2) their worldview emerges from the margins of society; (3) their identity is rooted in a belief that we share a common humanity; and (4) they embrace an ethics of revolution that demands structural change. Chapter two focuses on the role of religious faith in the lives of faith-inspired social-justice activists and offers brief spiritual biographies of Dietrich Bonhoeffer, Malcolm X, and Aung San

Suu Kyi. The next six chapters are three couplets looking at the themes of worldview, identity, and revolutionary ethics. Chapters three, five, and seven are biographical sketches—social science portraits—of the three principal leaders. I chose a different theme as a lens to look at each of the life stories. I use the theme of *worldview* to look at Bonhoeffer; *identity* to look at Malcolm X; and *ethics* to view Suu Kyi.

In chapters four, six, and eight, I closely examine these same three essentially spiritual themes by creating a conversation of sorts between Bonhoeffer, Malcolm X, Suu Kyi and other mystic-activists from the twentieth century, as well as with an assortment of theologians, theorists, and commentators. The ninth chapter returns to the discussion of the religious faith of mystic-activists with a few thoughts about the development of twenty-first-century faith-inspired leaders. The book concludes with an epilogue on religion and reconciliation in the twenty-first century. Brief biographies of the other twentieth century activists noted in this book can be found in the appendix.

I delve deeply into the lives and words of faith-inspired leaders who worked for social change in the twentieth century. My goal is to show how they became people who challenged society and effected change. I believe that this knowledge is important for the formation of twenty-first-century leaders. New leaders need to be equipped for interaction with a greater number of worldviews than previous generations as the diverse perspectives in our world increasingly meet.

In addition to his many literary works in the 1960s and 1970s, James Baldwin was also an acclaimed social critic. In an essay reflecting on the deaths of Malcolm X and Martin Luther King Jr. he sounds a warning: "The American republic has always done everything in its power to destroy our children's heroes, with the clear (and sometimes clearly stated) intention of destroying our children's hope. This endeavor has doomed the American nation: mark my words."[17] Baldwin's candid words of grief and despair spoke for the feelings of people all around the world. Like him, we can feel overwhelmed by the tragedy of ethnic hostilities, the gap between rich and poor, by individual and national choices that lead to chaos and social destabilization. We can "doom" our world as Baldwin warned. Our future on planet Earth depends greatly on the spirit of the leadership that emerges in this new century. Rather than allowing despair to paralyze us, we can choose to embrace the possibility of becoming a global community guided by justice and peace. By penning this book, I choose hope and the faith that leads to peace and justice.

2

THE JUST SHALL LIVE BY FAITH

In the twentieth century, Dietrich Bonhoeffer, Malcolm X, and Aung San Suu Kyi each demonstrated a vision for social justice rooted in their religious faith. Bonhoeffer was a Lutheran pastor who struggled in Germany against Adolf Hitler and the rise of Nazism. He warned of the dangers in this fascist philosophy and its obsessive anti-Semitism. Bonhoeffer grappled with new ways of comprehending God and God's relationship to humanity. He then invited others to join him in acting on those new understandings. On Hitler's orders, Bonhoeffer's voice was silenced by Nazi execution on April 9, 1945—just four weeks before Germany's surrender during World War II.

Malcolm X was a Muslim minister who struggled in the United States against racism. He protested the economic, social, and cultural impoverishment of urban African Americans and the damaging psychological effects of racism. He denounced an inhumane, racist, white power structure that had benefited from the systematic oppression of African Americans for over four hundred years. Malcolm X was a truth teller and invited anyone listening to join him in living according to that truth. Gunshots from rival Black Muslims silenced Malcolm X's voice on February 21, 1965.

Aung San Suu Kyi was a tireless champion for democracy in the struggle against tyranny in Burma (renamed Myanmar by the military leadership) during the final decades of the twentieth century. She found strength and inspiration in Buddhism. Suu Kyi's political party won the national elections in 1990, but the military refused to allow the democratically elected government to assume power. The military dictatorship placed her under house arrest just prior to the election, where she remains in 2007. Suu Kyi continues to speak out against oppression and repression while pleading for truth, freedom, reconciliation, and social justice.

Dietrich Bonhoeffer, Malcolm X, and Aung San Suu Kyi were inspired, guided, shaped, consoled, and empowered by their religious faith. I now examine the religious faith of mystic-activists—a faith rooted in the Scriptural call for peace and justice in the major religions of the world, and a faith experienced in moments of conversion and expressed in lives of spiritual practice.

Scripture Tradition

The sacred writings and narratives of the major faith groups call for justice. They give voice to the cry of oppressed people. Often, people who claim to follow the Scriptures of their faith tradition do not act as if they have heard those cries. But for those who embrace a divine agenda for social justice and reconciliation, their Scriptures contain "the seeds of radical, dramatic, critical evaluation of and action against an unjust social order."[1] Judaism, Christianity, and Islam are monotheistic religions that embrace similar views of God's mandate for reconciliation and social justice. The Hebrew Scriptures remind Jews that they know both oppression and liberation in their history. As the writer of Deuteronomy proclaims: "You shall not abuse a needy and destitute laborer, whether a fellow countryman or a stranger in one of the communities of your land.... You shall not subvert the rights of a stranger or the fatherless; you shall not take a widow's garment in pawn. Remember that you were a slave in Egypt and that the LORD your God redeemed you from there" (Deut 24:14, 17-18). The prophet Isaiah tells followers of God, "Learn to do good. Devote yourself to justice; aid the wronged. Uphold the rights of the orphan; defend the cause of the widow" (Isa 1:17). The writer of Proverbs bluntly states, "He who mocks the poor affronts his Maker" (Prov 17:5). Later the Talmud sums up the message of the Hebrew Scriptures: "What is hateful to yourself do not to your fellowman. That is the whole of the Torah and the remainder is but commentary. Go, learn it" (*Sabb.* 31A).[2]

Many Christians accept the guidance of the Hebrew Scriptures regarding reconciliation and social justice. The New Testament reinforces this mandate. Jesus states in his inaugural sermon: "The Spirit of the Lord is upon me, because he has anointed me to preach good news to the poor. He has sent me to proclaim release to the captives and recovery of sight to the blind, to let the oppressed go free, to proclaim the year of the Lord's favor.... Today this scripture has been fulfilled in your hearing" (Luke 4:18–19, 21). The apostle Paul interprets the death and resurrection of Jesus as creating a spiritual reality of justice and equality: "There is no longer Jew nor Greek, there is no longer slave or free, there is no longer male and female, for all of you are one in Christ Jesus" (Gal 3:28). The author of 1 John, like the writer of Proverbs in the Hebrew Scriptures, declares bluntly God's concern for justice: "How does God's love abide in anyone who has the world's goods and sees a brother or sister in need and yet refuses help?" (1 John 3:17).[3]

Islam makes social justice a central concern. The Qur'an witnesses to God's desire for justice: "Allah loves those who are fair and just" (49:9). In another place, the Qur'an elevates the importance of serving the poor. "How will you comprehend what the steep ascent is?—To free the neck (from the burden of debt or slavery), or to feed in times of famine the orphan near in relationship, or the poor in distress" (90:12–16). In the tradition of Proverbs and 1 John, the Qur'an also offers a blunt assessment of the person who resists the work of charity and social justice: "Have you seen him who denies the Day of Judgment? It is he who pushes the orphan away, and does not induce others to feed the needy" (107:1–3).[4]

Hinduism and Buddhism do not share a monotheistic understanding of God with Judaism, Christianity, and Islam. Nonetheless, these faiths also present a mandate for believers to work for social justice and reconciliation. In Hinduism's Bhagavad Gita, the god Krishna declares, "I am the same to all beings. With Me there is none disfavored, none favored; but those who worship Me with devotion are in Me and I in them" (9:29). Later the Bhagavad Gita states, "Nonviolence, truth, slowness to wrath, the spirit of dedication, serenity, aversion to slander, tenderness to all that lives, freedom from greed, gentleness, modesty, freedom from levity, spiritedness, forgiveness, fortitude, purity, freedom from ill will and arrogance—these are to be found in one born with the divine heritage, O Bharata" (16:2-3).[5]

Buddhist Scriptures are also passionate in this regard: "A man is not just if he carries a matter by violence; no, he who distinguishes both right and wrong, who is learned and leads others, not by violence but justly and righteously, and who is guided by the Law (Dharma) and intelligent, he is called just" (Dhammapada 19:256-257). Sāntideva states in the Bodhicaryavatara, "May I avert the pain of hunger and thirst with showers of food and drink, May I become both drink and food in the intermediate aeons of famine. May I be an inexhaustible treasure for impoverished beings.... This is the inexhaustible treasure, alleviating poverty in the world" (3:8-9, 28).[6]

A scriptural mandate for social justice and reconciliation provided a foundation for the vision and activism of Dietrich Bonhoeffer, Malcolm X, and Aung San Suu Kyi. They each refer to the teaching of their Scriptures and sacred stories in their writings and speeches. Since Bonhoeffer was a pastor and theologian, he was trained to integrate Scripture into his sermons, teaching, and theological works. Yet many clergy and theologians with a similar education do not become peace and justice advocates. Jesus' Sermon on the Mount and death on the cross in the New Testament informed Bonhoeffer's call to work for peace and justice. "Peacemakers will bear the cross with their Lord, for peace was made at the cross."[7]

An ordained imam and serious student of both the Qur'an and the Bible, Minister Malcolm X declared in a speech, "The [Qur'an] compels the Muslim world to take a stand on the side of those whose human rights are being violated, no matter what the religious persuasion of the victims is. Islam is a religion which concerns itself with the human rights of all mankind, despite race, color, or creed. It recognizes all (everyone) as part of one human family."[8]

Aung San Suu Kyi is not an ordained clergy or monk. In her work, however, she often refers to Buddhist concepts and the actions and teachings of the Buddha. She is also well versed in the Bible, which as a child she read in Burmese to her Christian grandfather.

Many other mystic-activists engage with sacred texts and stories in their pilgrimage toward leadership in movements for social change. Mohandas Gandhi often quoted the Bhagavad Gita. Along with Malcolm X and Aung San Suu Kyi, Gandhi was a student of Scripture traditions other than his own. The Sermon on the Mount informed his understanding of nonviolence. Rigoberta Menchú uses Scripture to equip people for activism. "Our main weapon...is the Bible. We began to study the Bible as a text through which to educate our village."[9] Mystic-activists rely on inspired religious writings and holy narratives as a foundation for their activism.

Faith Experience—Conversion

In addition to the power of Scripture, the experience of religious faith propels mystic-activists into the work they do. Most engage in spiritual practices such as prayer and meditation for inspiration and encouragement. Some recount conversions, encounters, epiphany moments, and peak experiences that transform their faith into a call to action for social justice. This was true for Dorothy Day. "When the demonstration was over and I had finished writing my story, I went to the national shrine at the Catholic University on the feast of the Immaculate Conception. There I offered up a special prayer, a prayer which came with tears and with anguish, that some way would open up for me to use what talents I possessed for my fellow workers, for the poor."[10] She pointed to this moment as the beginning of her faith-inspired activism with and on behalf of the poor. Dietrich Bonhoeffer and Malcolm X described encounters with the divine that altered their life paths and pushed them toward lives and ministries that pursued social justice. I now examine their faith journeys.

Dietrich Bonhoeffer

Dietrich Bonhoeffer grew up in a family that practiced Christianity at home, with an occasional connection to the organized Lutheran church. His mother taught the children religion from the Bible. Even though the family had little contact with institutional religion, from early childhood Bonhoeffer decided that he wanted to be a minister and a theologian in the organized church. Bonhoeffer was confirmed in the Lutheran church at age fifteen and began his study of theology at seventeen. His faith during his teenage and early adult years could be described as more of an intellectual venture than a spiritual experience.

In his mid-twenties, after he had studied theology and entered the ministry, Bonhoeffer went through a conversion that his biographer and closest friend, Eberhard Bethge, called a "transition from theologian to Christian."[11] Bonhoeffer never spoke of it publicly and described this experience only briefly in letters to family members and friends.

> I plunged into work in a very unchristian way. An...ambition that many noticed in me made my life difficult.... Then something happened, something that has changed and transformed my life to the present day. For the first time I discovered the Bible...I had often preached, I had seen a great deal of the church, spoken and preached about—but I had not yet become a Christian.... I know that at that time I turned the doctrine of Jesus Christ into something of personal advantage for myself.... Also, I had never prayed, only prayed a very little. For all my loneliness, I was quite pleased with myself. Then the Bible, and in particular the Sermon on the Mount, freed me from that. Since then everything has changed. I have felt this plainly, and so have other people about me. It was a great liberation.... My calling is quite clear to me. What God will make of it I do not know.... I must follow the path. Perhaps it will not be such a long one.... I believe that the nobility of this calling will become plain to us only in the times and events to come. If only we can hold out![12]

Bonhoeffer notes that he studied theology and entered the ministry as though on a career path rather than consumed by faith in God. He refers to a transformation that occurred in his life after which he became passionate about the study of Scripture and the practice of prayer as ways to connect with God. His mention of the Sermon on the Mount as the source of his faith understanding is significant. This compilation of Jesus' teachings found in the Gospel of Matthew has inspired many people to connect their faith with social justice. The Hindu Mohandas Gandhi credited the Sermon on the Mount as a primary source of his passion for social justice and commitment to nonviolence. Likewise, Martin Luther King Jr. followed Gandhi's lead in his reading of the Sermon on the Mount. Bonhoeffer made the connection even clearer in a letter written to his brother Karl-Friedrich:

> I believe I know that inwardly I shall be clear and honest with myself only if I truly begin to take seriously the Sermon on the Mount. That is the only source of power capable of blowing up the whole phantasmagoria [that is, the Nazi illusion] once and for all.... There just happen to be things that are worth an uncompromising stand. And it seems to me that peace and social justice, or Christ himself, are such things.[13]

This turning point led Dietrich Bonhoeffer to embrace a life of peace and justice (and a pacifist perspective). Although Bonhoeffer did not discuss his conversion in public, it permeated the remainder of his life. His new dynamic faith is apparent in the books he wrote after his conversion: *Life Together* and *Discipleship*. *Life Together* focuses on the life of community and on spiritual disciplines. *Discipleship* challenges the follower of Jesus Christ to accept the Sermon on the Mount as a directive for living a life of reconciliation and social justice. Because such a committed life leads often to ridicule and suffering, Bonhoeffer called this the path of "costly grace" rather than "cheap grace."[14]

Malcolm X

Like Dietrich Bonhoeffer, Malcolm X (born Malcom Little in 1925) grew up in a religious home that kept a distance from institutional religion. Malcolm's father spoke in a number of churches to spread the word of Black Nationalism. He had embraced Afro-centric cultural and religious teachings through the ideas of Marcus Garvey and his Back-to-Africa movement. Malcolm's mother exposed her children to a number of Christian denominations and religious groups including Baptists, Pentecostals, Methodists, Jehovah's Witnesses, and Seventh-Day Adventists. Malcolm X's brother Wilfred Little comments that "we were always taught by our mother not to give ourselves to any religion, but to always believe in God, and practice it in a spiritual way, not in a religious way."[15] For a brief time as a teenager, Malcolm sang in the choir at a Baptist Church and attended community youth events at a Congregational Church.[16]

Malcolm as a teenager lost all interest in religion and instead pursued a life without God. He became involved in the street life of Boston and New York City and finally succumbed to the downward spiral of drugs, sexual promiscuity, and crime. He was arrested and sent to prison. In prison, he considered himself an atheist and spoke scornfully about religion and God. During Malcolm X's imprisonment, several of his family members joined a religious group called the Nation of Islam, sometimes called Black Muslims—a religion that includes some practices from traditional Islam, yet conflicts with it on many points. His brother Reginald Little sent Malcolm a letter. "Malcolm, don't eat any more pork, and don't smoke any more cigarettes. I'll show you how to get out of prison."[17] Malcolm followed his brother's suggestions, thinking it was some sort of scheme for ending his incarceration, when his brother actually meant the prison of his own mind.

Soon Reginald (and later his sister Hilda) visited Malcolm X at the prison and told him about the beliefs of the Nation of Islam—a religion that strictly forbids sexual immorality, and prohibits eating pork or smoking cigarettes, among other things. He told Malcolm X, "There's a *man* who knows everything. God is a man. His real name is Allah." Reginald informed his brother that God came to the United States and revealed himself to a black man named Elijah Muhammad saying that the devil's days were about over. "The devil is also a man.... The white man is the devil."[18] During prison visits, Malcolm X's siblings taught him the beliefs of the Nation of Islam. Malcolm X was attracted by the idea that whites are devils, which resonated with his experience. He was also drawn by a religion for black people that reclaimed their African history and culture.

His family encouraged him to pray to Allah. Malcolm X later reflected on this challenge: "The hardest test I ever faced in my life was praying. You understand. My comprehending, my believing the teachings of Mr. Muhammad had only required my mind's saying to me, 'That's right!' or 'I never thought of that.' But bending my knees to pray—that act—well, that took me a week."[19] The process was very difficult for him. "For evil to bend its knees, admitting its guilt, to implore the forgiveness of God, is the hardest thing in the world. It's easy for me to see and to say that now. But then, when I was the personification of evil, I was going through it. Again, again, I would force myself back down into the praying-to-Allah posture."

Malcolm X experienced a dramatic change in his life. "I still marvel at how swiftly my previous life's thinking pattern slid away from me, like snow off a roof. It is as though someone else I knew of had lived by hustling and crime. I would be startled to catch myself thinking in a remote way of my earlier self as another person."[20] Malcolm X was a new person. His conversion to the Nation of Islam consumed the next sixteen years of his life.

In the early 1960s, Malcolm X privately began to question the Nation of Islam. He was convinced that his faith was in Allah, but the teachings and practices of the Nation of Islam contradicted those of traditional Islam. He felt drawn to Sunni Islam, the largest form of Islam. Malcolm X left the Nation of Islam in 1964. He immediately began to reorient himself towards orthodox Islam. In order to complete this process he went on the hajj, the pilgrimage to Mecca expected of all Muslims who are physically and financially able. This led to a second and more profound conversion experience. Malcolm arrived in Mecca, as did other pilgrims, dressed simply—wrapped in two white towels and wearing sandals. With thousands of other pilgrims, he participated in the rituals and prayers of the hajj, which includes walking seven times around the Kaaba. In a letter from the Holy Land sent to several family members and friends in the United States, he described his experience of conversion:

> I have been blessed to visit the Holy City of Mecca.... There were tens of thousands of pilgrims, from all over the world. They were of all colors, from blue-eyed blonds to black-skinned Africans. But we were all participating in the same ritual, displaying a spirit of unity and brotherhood that my experiences in America had led me to believe never could exist between the

white and the non-white. America needs to understand Islam, because this is the one religion that erases from its society the race problem. Throughout my travels in the Muslim world, I have met, talked to, and even eaten with people who in America would have been considered "white"—but the "white" attitude was removed from their minds by the religion of Islam. I have never before seen *sincere* and *true* brotherhood practiced by all colors together, irrespective of their color. You may be shocked by these words coming from me. But on this pilgrimage, what I have seen, and experienced, has forced me to *re-arrange* much of my thought-patterns previously held, and to *toss aside* some of my previous conclusions.[21]

Malcolm X was radically transformed by the Mecca experience and the teachings of traditional Islam. He discarded his views on race that classified whites as inherently evil devils. "I think that the pilgrimage to Mecca broadened my scope probably more in twelve days than my previous experience during my thirty-nine years on this earth."[22]

Faith Experience—Spiritual Practices

Conversion experiences or epiphany moments are not the only ways that mystic-activists connect with their faith. Many speak of spiritual practices such as prayer, fasting, and meditation that enable them to persevere in the struggle, gain clarity in vision, and obtain guidance for action. Like conversion experiences, spiritual disciplines transform the lives of faith-inspired leaders. Many different practices have been considered spiritual disciplines. Religion, spiritual teachers, and personal preference dictate these variations. Mystic-theologian Howard Thurman reflected on the power found in living a life formed by contemplation and spiritual discipline.

> The cruel vicissitudes of the social situation in which I have been forced to live in American society have made it vital for me to seek resources, or a resource, to which I could have access as I sought means for sustaining the personal enterprise of my life beyond all of the ravages inflicted upon it by the brutalities

of the social order. To live under siege, with the equilibrium and tranquility of peace, to prevent the springs of my being from being polluted by the bitter fruit of the climate of violence, to hold and re-hold the moral initiative of my own action and to seek the experience of community, all of this to whatever extent it has been possible to achieve it, is to walk through a door that no man can shut.[23]

For some, a spiritual life draws them closer to the earth and provides a way of sustaining an inner equilibrium. Winona LaDuke, an environmentalist and activist for Native American rights, speaks of how her faith strengthens her own resolve: "I find that trying to change this society is very consuming. And you have to always balance internal and external, so you have to work at doing it consciously. My ability to face the big external challenges is totally affected by my ability to retain my own spiritual relationship to the earth, as well as my own integrity. That kind of balance is a difficult piece."[24]

Other mystic-activists listen for a word from the divine or an inner voice through meditation and prayer. On one occasion, when Gandhi was working to remove the stigma and segregation of the "untouchable" class in Indian society, he heard an inner voice tell him that he needed to engage in a public fast. "At about twelve o'clock in the night something wakes me up suddenly, and some voice—within or without, I can not say—whispers, 'Thou must go on a fast.' 'How many days?' I ask. The voice again says, 'Twenty-one days.' 'When does it begin?' I asked. It says, 'You begin tomorrow.' I went off to sleep after making the decision."[25]

Mystic-activists also practice spiritual disciplines within a community of people of faith. The communal aspect of spirituality is essential if one desires to create a sense of common humanity in the broader society. Most faith-inspired activists participate in worship and community at a church, synagogue, mosque, temple, or a retreat center. Dietrich Bonhoeffer's conversion through the Sermon on the Mount led to a change in his practices. After his conversion experience, he regularly engaged in worship, community life, meditation, and prayer. The source of his "spiritual stamina and vitality [was] his constant, daily, childlike relationship to God."[26] A friend captured the humble essence of Bonhoeffer's faith: "One did not notice the solitude which prepared him for fellowship, the discipline which sustained his abandon, the quiet piety which nourished the acumen of his lively mind."[27]

Malcolm X also practiced the spiritual disciplines of his faith, observing the moral code of the Nation of Islam: "no drinking, no smoking, no drugs, no sexual license or even dating, no dances or ballgames or movies, no sleeping late, no more than one meal a day."[28] He continued in his commitment to religious practice when he converted to traditional Islam. "In Islam we practice prayer, charity, fasting. These should be practiced in all religions. The Muslim religion also requires one to make the pilgrimage to the Holy City of Mecca. I was fortunate enough to make it in April, and I went back again in September. Insofar as being a Muslim is concerned, I have done what one is supposed to do to be a Muslim."[29] Malcolm X's protégé, Benjamin Karim, was at Malcolm's home some nights and would "follow him up the stairs to his study in the attic, where Malcolm spent most of the time that he wasn't at the mosque. Malcolm's attic room told you this was a place where someone worked and thought." Karim observed that "just before dawn Malcolm would again be up so that he could say his first prayers at sunrise."[30]

Aung San Suu Kyi

The faith experience of Aung San Suu Kyi is best understood as spiritual discipline. Born in 1945, Suu Kyi was raised a devout Buddhist, yet "unlike many of her fellow Asians, she regards Buddhism not just as an inherited religion, but as a living faith that must be carefully cultivated and mastered through study and practice."[31] Although Aung San Suu Kyi grew up in a religious home, her practice of meditation was sporadic until she was thrust into leadership in the Burmese freedom movement. "I never really meditated very much. My real meditation took off only during my years of house arrest."[32] Every day she "rose at half past four in the morning and started with an hour of meditation" while under house arrest.[33] She explains that "meditation is a form of cultivating inner strength. And inner strength means inner peace. If you acquire inner strength that means that you are in a position to be able to face the troubles of the external world. And in that way, you can create your own sense of security, which comes from your inner strength. So, therefore, you are creating your own peace, as it were."[34]

Aung San Suu Kyi sums up the singular importance of a spiritual life for mystic-activists: "Our lives take on a rhythm different from those who, on waking up in the morning, do not need to wonder who might have been arrested during the night and what further acts of blatant injustice might be committed against our people later during the day. Our antennae become highly sensitive to vibrations barely noticed by those whose everyday existence is removed from political struggle." Suu Kyi continues, "The spiritual dimension becomes particularly important in a struggle in which deeply held convictions and strength of mind are the chief weapons against armed repression."[35]

Mystic-activists have a unique power as a result of their faith. They disturb "the status quo and traditional tranquility of the power structure." They also "question dominant societal values or ideological principles and the ruling elite's use of power or wealth and frequently achieve a following and through it generate pressure for major social change."[36] Their faith repeatedly influences both those who follow and work with them and the forces aligned against them.

Dietrich Bonhoeffer, 1944

© Chr. Kaiser/Gütersloher Verlagshaus, Germany

3

DIETRICH BONHOEFFER: "THE VIEW FROM BELOW"

In his last few years of life, Dietrich Bonhoeffer practiced and preached a way of understanding the world he called "the view from below."[1] He looked at society from the vantage point of those who were oppressed. His encounters with persons forced to the margins of society had transformed his worldview. Shortly before the Nazis imprisoned him, Bonhoeffer wrote of this way of seeing the world: "There remains an experience of incomparable value. We have for once learnt to see the great events of world history from below, from the perspective of the outcast, the suspects, the maltreated, the powerless, the oppressed, the reviled—in short, from the perspective of those who suffer."[2] When he wrote these words, this approach to world realities had already been his hermeneutic, or method of interpretation, for some time.

This view from below was quite a departure from Bonhoeffer's early years. He was born in Germany on February 4, 1906. His highly educated parents came from elite families who lived lives of privilege. His father was a respected professor of neurology and psychology in Berlin during much of Bonhoeffer's life. The Bonhoeffer family lived in an upscale neighborhood and enjoyed the benefits of "a private governess, music lessons, and a vacation home in the Harz Mountains."[3] Young Dietrich lived in a "happy and protected" home, which he later felt "sheltered him from some of the darker sides of life and isolated him from those less fortunate in society."[4]

Bonhoeffer's family was religious. Yet their faith was disengaged from issues of social justice. Bonhoeffer's decision to study theology and prepare for pastoral ministry in the church was not motivated by a passion for social justice. He enrolled in university studies at age seventeen, began his doctoral dissertation at age nineteen, and by age twenty-one had earned a doctorate in theology. This was followed by a brief period during which Bonhoeffer worked on a second dissertation and taught theology at the University of Berlin. His later view from below seems disconnected from his childhood and formal education.

Bonhoeffer first observed poverty during a short stint as an associate pastor at a congregation in Barcelona, Spain. This congregation was made up of many working class Germans living in Spain who were experiencing the harsh realities of economic depression. Having gained some experience with the personal impact of poverty, Bonhoeffer connected it to Scripture. In one sermon, he preached about how God was concerned with "those who are ever neglected, insignificant, weak, ignoble, unknown, inferior, oppressed, despised." His sermon ended by declaring that Christianity reverses the viewpoint of the world by witnessing to "the unending worth of the apparently worthless and the unending worthlessness of what is apparently so valuable."[5] A coming shift in his worldview would soon open his eyes to injustice as they had been opened to poverty.

Studying in the United States

A year in New York City was to be pivotal for the transformation of Dietrich Bonhoeffer's worldview. He was granted a fellowship to study at Union Theological Seminary, beginning in the fall of 1930. The academic rigor of seminaries in the United States did not impress him, compared to his German theological training. But he did have the opportunity to engage with the "social gospel"—a form of theology that demanded a commitment to social justice. At Union Seminary, he became friends with an African American student named Albert "Frank" Fisher. Through this friendship, Bonhoeffer gained an insider's view of the racial injustice in the United States and witnessed the worldview of persons victimized by racism.

Frank Fisher completed his pastoral field experience by serving as a minister at the historic Abyssinian Baptist Church in Harlem— a section of New York City that is a cultural Mecca for African Americans. Senior Pastor Adam Clayton Powell Sr. was a significant leader in the struggle against racial injustice.[6] Bonhoeffer joined Fisher on Sundays and participated in the life of the congregation, first by attending Sunday worship services and later by teaching Sunday school and Bible classes. He was often in the homes of church members. Bonhoeffer considered the preaching at Abyssinian Baptist Church and other African American congregations the most biblically authentic he heard while in the United States. "Here the Gospel of Jesus Christ, the savior of the sinner, is really preached and accepted with great welcome and visible emotion."[7]

Bonhoeffer spent a lot of time getting to know the Harlem community and the concerns of African Americans in general. He acquired publications from the National Association for the Advancement of Colored People (NAACP), read books by noted African American authors and collected recordings of African American spirituals composed during the slavery era. A fellow student from Union Seminary recalled, "What was so impressive was the way in which he pursued the understanding of the problem to its minutest detail through books and countless visits to Harlem, through participation in Negro youth work, but even more through a remarkable kind of identity with the Negro community, so that he was received there as though he had never been an outsider at all."[8]

Bonhoeffer eagerly immersed himself in many aspects of the African American experience of the 1930s. Frank Fisher also took him to African American communities in Philadelphia, Pennsylvania, and Washington, D.C. While in Washington, D.C., they visited Howard University, a premiere institution of higher learning in the African American community. On one occasion, Fisher was not given good service at a restaurant because of his race. Bonhoeffer left the establishment with Fisher.

The racial segregation of the church in the United States troubled Dietrich Bonhoeffer. He was concerned by the growing disillusionment among young African Americans whose parents had accommodated discrimination. Bonhoeffer believed that if the younger generation of African Americans left the Christian faith "white America would have to acknowledge its guilt."[9] The white church leaders' lack of concern regarding racism also offended him. "If it has come about that today the 'black Christ' has to be led into the field against the 'white Christ' by a young Negro poet, then a deep cleft in the church of Jesus Christ is indicated."[10] Listening to his recordings of spirituals, Bonhoeffer knew they were born out of racism. He marveled that these songs of struggle and liberation were popular in a white racist society: "Every white American knows, sings and loves these songs. It is barely understandable that great Negro singers can sing these songs before packed audiences of whites, to tumultuous applause, while at the same time these same men and women are still denied access to the white community through social discrimination."[11] Bonhoeffer believed that "the solution to the Negro problem is one of the decisive future tasks of the white churches."[12]

When Bonhoeffer prepared to leave the United States, Fisher said, "Make our sufferings known in Germany, tell them what is happening to us, and show them what we are like."[13] In Germany, Bonhoeffer did share with his students and fellow ministers his glimpses of African American life. The biggest impact the African American experience would have on the ministry of Dietrich Bonhoeffer was through the lens it gave him to view the racism in his own country—racism against people of Jewish descent.

Embracing the Perspective of Jews in Germany

When Bonhoeffer returned to Germany, he was ordained a Lutheran minister, and he accepted a position as a lecturer in theology at the University of Berlin. During this period, the Nazi (National Socialist) party was growing in influence, and Adolf Hitler was elected to office. The Bonhoeffer family was unhappy with the anti-Semitism of the Nazis and the Nazi leader's increasing power.

Hitler became chancellor of Germany on January 30, 1933. By this time, he had taken for himself the title *Führer* ("leader"). Two days later, in a previously scheduled radio address on the subject "The Younger Generation's Altered View of the Concept of the Führer,"

Bonhoeffer spoke of the dangers of idolizing the leader. His microphone was turned off before he could complete his message, which ended with the words, "Leaders or offices which set themselves up as gods mock God."[14] It is unknown whether the Nazis had control of the radio station or if Bonhoeffer had simply gone over his time. But he had carefully timed his message and read from a script. It was an eerie foretaste of things to come.

The Nazis immediately began to consolidate power and pursue their agenda after Hitler was named chancellor. Within a few months, the first concentration camp was set up in Dachau. The active persecution of Jews began.

The Bonhoeffer family had relationships with many persons of Jewish descent. More Jews lived in their Berlin neighborhood than other areas in the country. Yet the Bonhoeffers' liberal view "utterly disregarded racial origins, as long as one embraced Christian German culture."[15] There is no record of the Bonhoeffers having "any contact with religiously observant Jews or Jews of the ghetto."[16]

On April 1, 1933, a national boycott of Jewish-owned businesses was held. Julia Bonhoeffer, Dietrich's ninety-one-year-old grandmother, ignored the boycott and defiantly walked right past Nazi troops to shop at her usual Jewish-owned store. A German military officer standing outside the shop allegedly asked her, "Do you really have to buy from this Jew of all people?" The ninety-one-year-old hit his boots with her cane, pushed passed the guard, and said, "I will buy my butter where I always buy my butter."[17] Julia Bonhoeffer was the only one to shop at the store that day.

Just a few days later, persons with Jewish heritage were fired from their positions as civil servants and lawyers with the implementation of the Aryan Clause, which declared that persons of Jewish descent could not hold employment in government positions. Soon all Jews were barred from professional employment. Given that a large portion of the Protestant churches in Germany were part of the state church, the Aryan Clause also affected who could hold positions as pastors and theologians. Some German Jews had become Christians, and their positions in the church were threatened.

Adolf Hitler appointed a little known military chaplain, Ludwig Muller, as his liaison to the Protestant churches in late April. This was a first step in Hitler's attempt to take over the church in Germany. Church leaders sympathetic to the Nazis called themselves the German Christian Movement. A pamphlet circulated by the Nazis stated: "Without Hitler there is no National Socialism; without National Socialism there is no Third Reich; without the Third Reich there is no German Christian Movement; without the German Christian Movement there is no German Evangelical Church."[18] The rise of Hitler and the Nazis led to a marriage of nationalism and Christianity, with claims "that divine revelation worked through the emergence of Hitler."[19] Nazi propoganda caused a significant increase in Sunday church attendance.

In an unprecedented move, Ludwig Muller was elected the bishop of the German Protestant church in a manipulated election. His election allowed Hitler to "take Christianity under his firm protection."[20] Empowered by Hitler, Bishop Muller became the *Führer* of the church—a Nazi Reich bishop. He modeled his leadership style after Adolf Hitler himself and wielded powers never before exercised in the church in Germany. In the days, months, and years that followed, under Muller's orders, the Nazification of the church was all-encompassing. German Christian synod delegates wore armbands with the Nazi swastika symbol. Youth groups were combined into the Hitler Youth organization. The church produced anti-Semitic literature and removed Christians of Jewish ancestry from the ranks of pastor and the rolls of church membership. The Hebrew Bible (Old Testament) was discarded. A new version of the New Testament was prepared that eliminated all references to the Hebrew Scriptures and any suggestion that Jesus might be Jewish. The new version sold two hundred thousand copies. An ethnically cleansed hymnal and catechism were also published.[21]

Many church leaders were distressed by Hitler's intervention into church life. But few spoke out against it, partly because they were encouraged at how the Nazis were reviving the nation's morale and economy. And Nazi anti-Semitism was far from foreign to much of Christianity, which had a long anti-Semitic history, based on church teachings that Jews were guilty as a race for the death of Christ.

A small group of pastors, including Dietrich Bonhoeffer, did voice dissent shortly before the elevation of Ludwig Muller to bishop.

This group of ministers formed the Pastors Emergency League to protest Nazi influence on the church and the potentially heretical views that were being introduced to accommodate the Nazi agenda. There was disagreement within this group about what needed to be challenged. All agreed that it was untenable for the church to be under the sway of the Nazis and that Hitler's intention to install a Nazi bishop was even worse. Bonhoeffer was also greatly disturbed by the Nazi's strong anti-Semitic attitudes and actions. The group asked Bonhoeffer and another theologian to draft a statement of faith for the Pastors Emergency League. The draft of the Bethel Confession renounced both the Nazi attempt to influence and control the church and the government's treatment of Jews. The statement was presented to twenty theologians who proceeded to delete most of the radical elements—particularly those concerning the plight of Jews. Bonhoeffer refused to sign the final document.

Dietrich Bonhoeffer was often alone among Christian leaders in his concern for what was happening to Jews in Germany. Shortly after the boycott of Jewish-owned businesses and the announcement of the Aryan Clause, Bonhoeffer published an article entitled, "The Church and the Jewish Question." In a letter, Bonhoeffer noted that most church leaders refused to take the threat to Jews seriously. He wrote, "The Jewish question troubles the church very much and here even the most intelligent people have entirely lost their heads and their Bibles over it."[22] Many Christians in Germany during the 1930s were prejudiced against Jews. So they considered Bonhoeffer irrelevant and scandalous when he wrote, "What is at stake is by no means the question whether our German members of congregations can still tolerate church fellowship with the Jews. It is rather the task of Christian preaching to say: here is the church, where Jew and German stand together under the Word of God; here is the proof whether a church is still the church or not."[23]

Bonhoeffer identified three responsibilities the church should fulfill in its relationship with the state. First, the church "can ask the state whether its actions are legitimate." Second, "The church has an unconditional obligation to the victims of any ordering of society, even if they do not belong to the Christian community." He was making the case that the church had to reach out to victims of government actions, whether they were Christians or not. In this case, it was a direct plea to stand with the Jews. Bonhoeffer continued:

> The third possibility is not just to bandage the victims under the wheel, but to put a spoke in the wheel itself. Such action would be direct political action, and is only possible and desirable when the church sees the state fail in its function of creating law and order.[24]

When he read his article at a monthly gathering of pastors, his comments about political action so disturbed listeners that some got up and left. German theologian Heinz Eduard Tödt said, "In 1933, Bonhoeffer was almost alone in his opinions; he was the only one who considered solidarity with the Jews, especially with the non-Christian Jews, to be a matter of such importance as to obligate the Christian churches to risk a massive conflict with that state—a risk which could threaten their very existence."[25]

Although Bonhoeffer's article was radical in his time and setting, he was still struggling with his own prejudice against Jews. A residue of that prejudice can be observed if the article is read in full. His use of language such as the "Jewish question" or "Jewish problem" illustrates that he still viewed Jews as *other* rather than as *us*. The phrases imply that the problem resided with the Jewish people themselves, rather than in the anti-Semitism of many Germans and the institutions of the nation.[26]

An even more revealing incident happened in that same month of April 1933. Bonhoeffer's twin sister Sabine was married to Gerhard Leibholz, who was of Jewish lineage. Leibholz's presence in the family was a constant personal reminder of the impact of growing anti-Semitism in German society. On April 11, Leibholz's father died, and the family asked Bonhoeffer to officiate at the funeral. Since the father was not baptized, Bonhoeffer thought he should confer with his general superintendent in the church. Bonhoeffer was told that it was not a good time to officiate at a funeral for a Jew. So he declined. The bold Bonhoeffer who challenged his church leaders and the government on the "Jewish Question" lost his courage in this matter.

He quickly regretted his decision. In November of the same year, he wrote his brother-in-law:

> I am tormented by the thought... that I didn't do as you asked me as a matter of course. To be frank, I can't think what made me behave as I did. How could I have been so much afraid at the time? It must have seemed equally incomprehensible to all of you, and yet you said nothing. But it preys on my mind... because it's the kind of thing one can never make up for. So all I can do is to ask you to forgive my weakness then. I know now for certain that I ought to have behaved differently.[27]

Bonhoeffer's twin sister and her family later fled to England due to the persecution of Jews in Germany. By that time, Bonhoeffer's courage was more consistent and his advocacy on behalf of Germany's Jewish citizens also placed him in harm's way. His words and actions grew bolder. When he spoke at international ecumenical gatherings, he raised the issue. After the Nuremberg Laws, which denied citizenship to Jews in Germany, were implemented in 1935, he proclaimed, "Only he who cries out for the Jews is permitted to sing Gregorian chants!"[28] This statement reveals Bonhoeffer's view that Christian faith clearly demanded that one must defend the Jews. To do otherwise or to remain silent was in effect a denial of one's faith in Christ.

Confessing Church

Bonhoeffer accepted an appointment as a pastor of a German-speaking congregation in London in October 1933. The weak version of the Bethel Confession approved by the Pastors Emergency League and the lack of commitment to address the racism of the Nazi government left Bonhoeffer disappointed with his church. He also found himself in London because there were no parishes in Berlin that wanted a pastor who was "so young, so radical, and so antagonistic toward the ideology of National Socialism."[29] Bonhoeffer himself recognized his isolation. He wrote his theological mentor Karl Barth regarding his decision to go to London:

I felt that I was incomprehensibly in radical opposition to all my friends, that my views of matters were taking me more and more into isolation, although I was and remained in the closest personal relationship with those men—and all that made me anxious, made me uncertain. I was afraid I would go wrong out of obstinacy—and I saw no reason why I should see these things more correctly, better than so many able and good pastors, to whom I looked up—and so I thought that it was probably time to go into the wilderness for a while.[30]

The Pastors Emergency League soon grew into what was called the Confessing Church—"so named because it claimed to be the 'true' Evangelical church of Germany doctrinally grounded in the confessions of the Reformation."[31] The Confessing Church was a grassroots association of pastors, laity, and theologians. The primary focus of this union of congregations was to resist Nazi attempts to control the organizational life and change the core theological underpinnings of the church. The Confessing Church proclaimed its autonomy from the government and its complete dependence on God alone for authority. For the remainder of Bonhoeffer's life, this would be his church.

The Confessing Church organized in May 1934 and issued the Barmen Confession, a document challenging the Nazi attempt to control the dogma and life of the church. The confession proclaimed, "We repudiate the false teaching that there are areas of our life in which we belong not to Jesus Christ but to other lords."[32] The Barmen Confession directly defied Hitler's attempt to co-opt the church in Germany. It was a bold statement for this small group of Lutheran pastors. After the publication of the Barmen Confession, the secret police closely monitored those who had signed it. Bonhoeffer had not been present for the meeting—he was a pastor in London at this point—but he was pleased by its strongly worded content. Unfortunately it still did not include the kind of support for the Jewish community Bonhoeffer desired.

The Lutheran Church in Germany traditionally supported the government as having a God-given role in society that was beyond critique. Bonhoeffer recognized the impotency of the mainstream

Protestant church in Germany, and its inability to challenge Hitler "revealed the problematic character of its entire past: its veneration of and obedience to the state, its support for the traditional class system, its resistance to social change, its indifference to the plight of workers and the poor, and its opposition to socialism and working class politics."[33]

Bonhoeffer remained committed to the Confessing Church despite his concern that it did not go far enough in its support for Jews. Further, he refused to attend any international meetings where the German Christian Movement (the majority of the church controlled by the Nazis) was invited to represent the church of Germany, even if the Confessing Church was also invited. In 1936 Bonhoeffer clarified his position when he said, "He who separates himself from the Confessing Church separates himself from salvation."[34]

Peacemaker

The Nazi regime also troubled Dietrich Bonhoeffer because of its warmongering ways. He believed that war was senseless and antithetical to the teachings of Jesus, particularly as found in the Sermon on the Mount. Bonhoeffer's initial encounters with pacifist Christians came while studying at Union Theological Seminary in New York. In addition to his friendship with Frank Fisher, he spent much time with Jean Lasserre, a student from France who was a pacifist. This was an unlikely friendship given the hostile relations between Germany and France at the time. Bonhoeffer's friendship with Lasserre led to further reflection on the Sermon on the Mount and a deepening of his faith. After Bonhoeffer's return to Germany, he expressed in many settings his commitment to peace. In 1932, he spoke to a group of students in Berlin where he connected their belief in Christ to becoming "witnesses for peace."[35] He made clear that witnessing for peace did not mean being passive. In another setting he proclaimed, "But the church also knows that there is no peace unless justice and truth are preserved. A peace which does damage to justice and truth is no peace, and the church of Christ must protest against such peace."[36]

Bonhoeffer's growing commitment to peace gave birth to a desire to spend time with Mohandas Gandhi in India. Letters were sent on behalf of Bonhoeffer to the Mahatma, the "great-soul," about a visit in early 1935. Soon a letter arrived from Gandhi:

> With reference to your desire to share my daily life, I may say that you will be staying with me if I am out of prison and settled in one place when you come. But otherwise, if I am traveling or if I am in prison, you will have to be satisfied with remaining in or near one of the institutions that are being conducted under my supervision. If you can live on the simple vegetarian food that these institutions can supply you, you will have nothing to pay for boarding and lodging.[37]

During the same period of time that he sought to meet Gandhi, Bonhoeffer was invited to speak at a conference in Fanö, Denmark. This conference, sponsored by the World Council of Churches, was held in August 1934. Bonhoeffer had been involved with the Ecumenical Movement and his voice was gaining credibility as a witness to what was happening in Germany. He used this opportunity to present a vision of the world church as peacemakers and defenders of the oppressed. He preached on the subject, "The Church and the Peoples of the World." His text was Psalm 85:8, "Let me hear what God the Lord will speak, for he will speak peace unto his people." Speaking in English, the twenty-eight-year-old Bonhoeffer challenged the conference delegates:

> This church of Christ lives at one and the same time in all peoples, yet beyond all boundaries, whether national, political, social, or racial.... For the members of the ecumenical church, in so far as they hold to Christ, his word, his commandment of peace is more holy, more inviolable that the most revered words and works of the natural world.... They cannot take up arms against Christ himself—yet this is what they do if they take up arms against one another!... For peace must be dared. It is the great venture. It can never be safe. Peace is the opposite of security. To demand guarantees is to mistrust, and this mistrust in turn brings forth war. To look for guarantees is to want to protect oneself. Peace means to give oneself altogether to the law

of God, wanting no security, but in faith and obedience laying the destiny of the nations in the hand of Almighty God, not trying to direct it for selfish purposes. Battles are won, not with weapons, but with God. They are won where the way leads to the cross. Which of us can say he knows what it might mean for the world if one nation should meet the aggressor, not with weapons in hand, but praying, defenseless, and for that very reason protected by "a bulwark never failing"?. . . Only the one great Ecumenical Council of the holy church of Christ over all the world can speak out so that the world, though it gnash its teeth, will have to hear, so peoples will rejoice because the church of Christ in the name of Christ has taken the weapons from the hands of their sons, forbidden war, proclaimed the peace of Christ against the raging world. . . . The Ecumenical Council is in session; it can send out to all believers this radical call to peace. . . . We want to give the world a whole word, not a half word—a courageous word, a Christian word.[38]

The delegates found Bonhoeffer's message exhilarating. Yet most of them were resigned to the reality of war in Europe. There was no clarion call for peace by the world church, and it would seem that "Bonhoeffer had leapt so far ahead of everyone else in the cause of peace that none were able to follow him."[39] With a world church that was unwilling, or believed itself unable, to take up his challenge, Bonhoeffer continued making plans to go to India.

The Illegal Seminaries of the Confessing Church

Dietrich Bonhoeffer would never go to India or meet Mohandas Gandhi. He gave up his dream of visiting India in order to lead a new seminary for the Confessing Church. The Nazis were taking control of the theological faculties in the universities and closed many seminaries. In order to provide training for clergy, the Confessing Church organized five preachers' seminaries. The seminaries were illegal because the Nazi regime had banned the Confessing Church. Therefore, these centers of theological study existed outside the realm of the Nazi state and relied on donations to operate. This underground existence offered the luxury of theological freedom and societal critique. Bonhoeffer returned to Germany from his pastorate in England to lead the Finkenwalde Seminary, which opened in 1935. The school would exist for just over two years before the Gestapo closed it. The seminary then continued less formally for a few more years. The Finkenwalde Seminary years were very fruitful for Dietrich Bonhoeffer, the theologian. Two of his most influential books in the life of the Christian church then (and now) were written: *Discipleship* and *Life Together*.

The pressures from the Nazi government on Confessing Church pastors did not let up. Many pastors and seminarians were arrested and imprisoned. In celebration of the Nazi leader's fiftieth birthday in 1939, all pastors were ordered to swear their loyalty to Hitler. To Bonhoeffer's dismay, nearly all of the Confessing Church pastors obeyed. By 1940, the military would draft into military service most of the pastors who were not in prison.

Kristallnacht

On the night of November 9, 1938, the Nazis unleashed a frenzy of hatred upon German Jews. In a state-sponsored act of terrorism, Nazi Party members and military forces smashed windows in Jewish homes and shops throughout Germany and Austria. They destroyed more than 7,500 Jewish-owned businesses. The shattered glass gave the night its name: Kristallnacht (Crystal Night). Nazis beat and terrorized countless citizens of Jewish descent, and murdered nearly one hundred more. They arrested tens of thousands more and sent them to concentration camps. The anti-Semitic violence lasted twenty-four hours, during which the Nazis set synagogues on fire and desecrated hundreds of Torah scrolls.

The church remained silent in the midst of this travesty. Christians made no public protests. No pastors or priests condemned this attack on the Jewish community from their pulpits. Even among the Confessing Church, few church leaders spoke publicly against the brutality.

Dietrich Bonhoeffer went to Berlin to view firsthand the destruction his fellow Germans had wrought. He was enraged by the events and maintained "how reprehensible it was for Christians to make the connection, as many did, between the destruction of Jewish property and the so-called curse on Jews because of their alleged participation in the death of Christ."[40] Bonhoeffer by this time had shed as much as possible the remnants of the anti-Semitism he had grown up with. He embraced the righteous anger of God against the oppression of the Jews.

Bonhoeffer's friend Eberhard Bethge noticed in the Bible that Bonhoeffer used for his personal devotion that he had underlined a phrase in one of his beloved Psalms: "They said to themselves: 'We will utterly subdue them'; they burned all the meeting places of God in the land" (Ps 74:8). Next to the underlined verse, he wrote the date of Kristallnacht, "9.11.38!"—the ninth of November 1938.[41] Later Bonhoeffer discussed Kristallnacht with his seminarians. He shared an insight on how ethnic and religious bigotry operates: "If synagogues are set afire today, tomorrow the churches will burn."[42]

The persecution of Jews intensified. In 1941, the Nazis required Jews to wear a yellow star on their clothes to announce their heritage to all who came in contact with them. This public sign of their exclusion affected all aspects of life. Jews were pushed further to the margins. Even in the church, "when Christians of Jewish descent, who were considered Jewish under Nazi law, appeared with their yellow badges, some Aryan Christians complained that they did not want to pray or take communion next to Jews."[43] The persecution, removal to concentration camps, and systematic killing of Jews decimated the Jewish population in Germany. It fell from 500,000, before the rise of the Nazis, to 150,000 in late 1941.

Second Visit to the United States

In 1939, Bonhoeffer decided to leave Germany and return to the United States. War was looming, and Bonhoeffer knew he would soon face the draft. While ministers in the Confessing Church deplored Adolf Hitler and the Nazi government, if the call came to fight for Germany, they would respond. Many already had joined the military. Bonhoeffer's Christian pacifism did not allow him to serve in the military. He was also very discouraged by the state of the Confessing Church. The church had not lived up to his expectations as a prophetic voice and active force against the Nazis. Bonhoeffer was seeking a time of reflection and respite for his soul. He believed that the United States would also offer him a platform for informing the world about what was happening in Germany. He hoped, in particular, to appeal to the ecumenical church to speak out against the Nazis. Bonhoeffer's friends in the United States saw this as an opportunity to rescue him from the dangers of Germany and ensure a future for one of the church's most creative young theologians.

After some inquires, Dietrich Bonhoeffer received an invitation to teach a summer class at Union Theological Seminary, where he had studied nine years earlier. His plan was to stay in the United States not longer than a year. Shortly after his arrival, Bonhoeffer was haunted by doubts about whether he had made the right decision in leaving Germany. He wrote in his journal, "I do not understand why I am here, whether it was the sensible thing to do, whether the results will be worthwhile."[44]

After a few weeks of inner turmoil, he decided to return to Germany. He wrote theologian Reinhold Niebuhr, his host at Union Seminary:

> I have made a mistake in coming to America. I must live through this difficult period of our national history with the Christian people of Germany. I will have no right to participate in the reconstruction of Christian life in Germany after the war if I do not share the trials of this time with my people.... Christians in Germany will face the terrible alternative of either willing the defeat of their nation in order that Christian civilisation may survive, or willing the victory of their nation and thereby destroying our civilisation. I know which of these alternatives I must choose; but I cannot make that choice in security.[45]

Less than a month after arriving in New York City, Bonhoeffer was on his way back to Germany on the last ship to set sail before the start of World War II. It was the only decision his conscience would let him make. It would cost him his life.

Conspirator

Dietrich Bonhoeffer's life took a dramatic turn upon his return to Germany. He joined an underground conspiracy to assassinate Adolf Hitler. Members of the Bonhoeffer family were involved in this resistance movement. Hans von Dohnanyi, who was married to Dietrich's older sister Christine, had introduced Bonhoeffer to leaders of the resistance in 1938. Bonhoeffer's older brother Klaus and another brother-in-law, Rudiger Schleicher, were also involved. Leaders in the Abwehr, the counterintelligence wing of the German military, were at the core of the conspiracy against Hitler. Bonhoeffer became a civilian member of the Abwehr, which also protected him from draft into the military.

The primary role that Bonhoeffer played in the resistance was to use his contacts in the ecumenical church to provide information for the Allies. He traveled as a theologian on church business with the secret agenda of seeking support from other nations. The resistance hoped that if they could kill Hitler, the Allies would be ready to negotiate a settlement to the war with Germany.

The decision to kill was difficult for a pacifist who valued life and peace. Bonhoeffer biographer Edwin Robertson notes, "His involvement in the conspiracy would require the abandoning of much that Christian life demands—expert lying built up gradually into closely woven deception, and ultimately the willingness to kill. Not for a moment did he regard these evils as anything more than they were—evil. But he saw them as necessary."[46]

Bonhoeffer's choice required a personal faith able to make painful decisions in complex times—choices that would certainly be misunderstood and even seen as heretical. Eberhard Bethge wrote:

Bonhoeffer the theologian and Christian was entering fully into his contemporary world, his place, and his time—into a world his bourgeois class had helped to bring about rather than prevent. He accepted the burden of that collective responsibility, and began to identify himself with those who were prepared to acknowledge their guilt and to begin shaping something new for the future—instead of merely protesting on ideological grounds, as the church had done up to that point. In 1939 the theologian and Christian became a man for his times."[47]

As Bethge reflected on Bonhoeffer's decision, he noted the sacrifice that was required of his friend and fellow theologian—"the sacrifice of his Christian reputation." Yet Bethge understood this as an act of faith: "To want to be only a Christian, a timeless disciple—that now became a costly privilege. To become engaged for his times, where he stood, was far more open to misinterpretation, less glorious, more confined. Yet this alone was what it now meant to be a Christian."[48]

Bonhoeffer's life of faith began a strange dance. While with his pastor friends and theological colleagues, he lived and spoke as he always had. With fellow conspirators, he was an agent who secretly brought their message to the wider world. Bethge noted that Bonhoeffer's fellow church activists "felt there was something incognito about his existence that they mustn't question." When with the conspirators, "his Christian existence seldom emerged openly." Bethge added, "Whether among his old friends or new ones, he instinctively hid the other side of his being. Anyone who had anything to do with him sensed that there was more there than could be seen; but no one had the impression of any inner conflict. Everything was in order."[49]

A double life became Bonhoeffer's fate. He daily lived in the dual realities of theologian and conspirator, which presented him with some interesting choices. One afternoon in 1940, after a conference for the Confessing Church, Bonhoeffer and his friend Bethge—one of the few people aware of his double life—were sitting at an outdoor café. From a loudspeaker in the restaurant came the news that France had surrendered to Germany. The people in the café stood, raised their arms in the Nazi salute, and jubilantly began to sing patriotic songs. Bonhoeffer and Bethge also stood. Bethge described what happened next: "Bonhoeffer raised his arm in the regulation Hitler salute, while I stood there dazed. 'Raise your arm! Are you crazy?' he whispered to me, and later: 'We shall have to run risks for very different things now, but not for that salute!'"[50]

Bonhoeffer took on the role of conspirator in order to help the Jewish people. According to Bethge, "There is no doubt that Bonhoeffer's primary motivation for entering active political conspiracy was the treatment of the Jews by the Third Reich."[51] With family members holding important positions in the Abwehr, Bonhoeffer had seen details of the Nazi genocide of the Jews. The third point in his 1933 article on "The Church and the Jewish Question" had called for "direct political action." Seeing no other way to stop the onrushing Nazi machine, Bonhoeffer decided that he must join the efforts to jam a "spoke in the wheel itself." For Bonhoeffer, stopping the persecution and slaughter of Jews was at the core of his faith. He summed up his outlook in a stunningly clear statement from his unfinished manuscript *Ethics*: "An expulsion of the Jews from the west must necessarily bring with it the expulsion of Christ. For Jesus Christ was a Jew."[52] Bonhoeffer was seeing his faith with a view from below—with Jewish eyes.

Bonhoeffer struggled with the issue of responsibility in his attempt to understand why he felt compelled to join the conspiracy and what that meant for his life of faith. The more that he learned of the Nazi genocide of the Jews, the more he experienced the guilt of inaction. "I am guilty of cowardly silence at a time when I ought to have spoken. I am guilty of hypocrisy and untruthfulness in the face of force. I have been lacking in compassion and I have denied the poorest of my brethren."[53] As Bonhoeffer's outrage against injustice grew, and his actions came to match his passion, his awareness of guilt was transferred to the church collectively. "The Church confesses that she has witnessed the lawless application of brutal force, the physical and spiritual suffering of countless innocent people, oppression, hatred and murder, and that she has not raised her voice on behalf of the victims and has not found ways to hasten to their aid. She is guilty of the deaths of the weakest and most defenseless brothers of Jesus Christ."[54]

Bonhoeffer also accepted the possibility of guilt as a consequence of his choices. He noted that his actions "may prevent me from taking up my ministry again later on."[55] Bonhoeffer's view from the margins caused him to step outside the boundaries of traditional Christian forms of activism. On another occasion he wrote, "I became certain that the duty had been laid on me to hold out in this boundary situation with all its problems."[56] In a message to family and friends at Christmas in 1942, he reflected on the life he and others were living as conspirators: "We have been silent witnesses of evil deeds; we have been drenched by many storms; we have learned the arts of equivocation and pretense; experience had made us suspicious of others and kept us from being truthful and open; intolerable conflicts have worn us down and even made us cynical. Are we still of any use?"[57]

Bonhoeffer seems to have come to terms with his decision to work with the conspiracy: "The ultimate question for a responsible man to ask is not how he is to extricate himself heroically from the affair, but how the coming generation is to live. It is only from this question, with its responsibility towards history, that fruitful solutions can come, even if for the time being they are very humiliating."[58]

In the midst of his resistance work, Bonhoeffer became engaged to marry Maria von Wedemeyer. He and Maria had met while she was still a young child, the granddaughter of a patron and supporter of the Confessing Church seminary at Finkenwalde. They met again as adults and discovered a love for each other. Dietrich was thirty-six and Maria was eighteen. They seemed a good match, despite the age difference. Yet it took time for their relationship to become romantic. On January 13, 1943, Maria responded to Dietrich's invitation of marriage with a letter that said, "With all my happy heart, I can now say yes." But the letter began, "Dear Pastor Bonhoeffer."[59]

The Gestapo began an investigation to identify the members of the resistance. The attempts to assassinate Adolf Hitler greatly accelerated this process and many were under surveillance. The Gestapo discovered Bonhoeffer's name when they examined financial irregularities in the Abwehr and found the plans of the resistance movement. They tapped his phone.

Two more attempts on Hitler's life failed in March. On April 5, 1943, the Nazi government arrested Dietrich Bonhoeffer and his brother-in-law Hans von Dohnanyi. They sent Bonhoeffer to the Tegel Prison in Berlin where he was imprisoned in "a cell room, six by nine feet, characterized by the simplest and humblest of accommodations—a hard narrow bed, a shelf, a stool, a bucket, and a skylight window."[60] During two years of imprisonment, his captors interrogated him in ways that many would consider torture. He never was free again. He did not marry. Yet in prison, Bonhoeffer would write some of his most creative works.

Religionless Christianity

While in prison, Bonhoeffer reflected on the church through the lens of those who had suffered and died in Germany while the church had remained silent—or, even worse, had supported the Nazi regime. He struggled with the essence of his faith. What credibility did the institutional church have? What person with any integrity would want to follow Jesus when the church had embraced Adolf Hitler and approved of the oppression and murder of innocent people?

As Bonhoeffer pondered the evil in the human condition—and the fact that many of the perpetrators called themselves Christians— he became disillusioned with the idea of religion. He wrote his friend Eberhard Bethge from prison: "What is bothering me incessantly is the question what Christianity really is, or indeed who Christ really is, for us today.... We are moving towards a completely religion-less time; people as they are now simply cannot be religious any more. Even those who honestly describe themselves as 'religious' do not in the least act up to it, and so they presumably mean something quite different by 'religious.'"[61]

Bonhoeffer had seen a church that practiced the rites of religion but was unwilling to advocate for peace and justice in the world. He was concerned that the church of the postwar era might try to "convince itself that it was without blame for the atrocities of the Hitler years." Bonhoeffer knew at the very depths of his being that "the words of the churches had lost any claim to credibility" because of "the acts of injustice perpetrated by so-called Christians, abetted by their churches."[62]

In the desperation and disillusionment of his prison cell, Bonhoeffer began to consider the idea of a religionless Christianity. When Bonhoeffer called for a religionless Christianity, he was not divorcing himself from faith. Rather he was redefining faith. He wrote in a letter for his godson's baptism: "Our church, which has been fighting in these years only for its self-preservation, as though that were an end in itself, is incapable of taking the word of reconciliation and redemption to mankind and the world.... Our being Christians today will be limited to two things: prayer and action by the just person on behalf of people."[63] He envisioned a form of faith that would be needed in the future.

Bonhoeffer re-imagined faith in a world that had experienced an apathetic, corrupt, and sometimes even demonic religion. He noted distinctions between a religion that consisted only of the completion of rituals and one that relied on the authenticity of a lived faith. Faith must be lived in response to real life and suffering in the world. "It is not the religious act that makes the Christian, but participation in the sufferings of God in the secular life.... Jesus calls men, not to a new religion, but to life.... I'm still discovering right up to this moment, that it is only by living completely in this world that one learns to have faith."[64]

Final Days

Dietrich Bonhoeffer was kept at Tegel Prison for eighteen months. Then he was moved to another prison for four months, next to the Buchenwald concentration camp for seven weeks, and finally to the Flossenburg concentration camp. His interrogators intensified their methods during his final months. On April 5, 1945, two years after Bonhoeffer's arrest, Adolf Hitler ordered his execution.[65]

Dietrich Bonhoeffer's devotion to God shown forth in his final days. Another prisoner recalled, "He was one of the very few men I have ever met to whom his God was real and ever close to him."[66] On Sunday, April 8, Bonhoeffer led a service at the request of his fellow prisoners and spoke on the texts of the day: "By his bruises we are healed" (Isa 53:5) and "Blessed be the God and Father of our Lord Jesus Christ! By his great mercy he has given us a new birth into a living hope through the resurrection of Jesus Christ from the dead" (1 Pet 1:3).

Shortly after the service, the Gestapo arrived. Bonhoeffer asked a British prisoner if he somehow found his way back to England to pass on a message to his friend the bishop of Chichester, "This is the end—for me the beginning of life."[67] These were the last recorded words Dietrich Bonhoeffer spoke.

A Nazi court held a short trial and convicted Bonhoeffer of high treason. On April 9, 1945, Dietrich Bonhoeffer calmly walked to the gallows and was hung to death. Three weeks later, Adolf Hitler committed suicide. Germany surrendered less than a month after Bonhoeffer's death.

Dietrich Bonhoeffer wrote in his book *Discipleship*, "Whenever Christ calls us, his call leads us to death."[68] Bonhoeffer's call led to death in a concentration camp. His faith told him a Jew named Jesus had died so that he could be saved from his sins. His faith compelled him to risk death because he wanted to save persons of Jewish descent from the sins of the Nazis. When Dietrich Bonhoeffer wrote about his process of conversion he stated:

> My calling is quite clear to me. What God will make of it I do not know.... I must follow the path. Perhaps it will not be such a long one.... I believe that the nobility of this calling will become plain to us only in times and events to come.[69]

4

A WORLDVIEW FROM THE MARGINS

Dietrich Bonhoeffer was born into privilege. As his sheltered faith encountered the reality of human suffering at the margins of society, his elite worldview gradually transformed. He wrote of this metamorphosis, this new way of seeing the world: "There remains an experience of incomparable value. We have for once learnt to see the great events of world history from below, from the perspective of the outcast, the suspects, the maltreated, the powerless, the oppressed, the reviled—in short, from the perspective of those who suffer."[1] For Bonhoeffer, solidarity was not merely living with the oppressed or mirroring the experience of the powerless; it meant full immersion into their worldview. In other words, one with a view from below seeks to see the world as though he or she is actually the person being oppressed.

Bonhoeffer's life educated his way of seeing and thinking. His faithful response to God's call to justice led him to understand the importance of solidarity with the oppressed—and it eventually cost him his life. Latin American liberation theologian Gustavo Gutiérrez wrote that Bonhoeffer experienced an "apprenticeship" that caused him to move "toward a theological outlook whose departure is in a faith lived by exploited classes, condemned ethnic groups, and marginalized cultures."[2] People living at the margins of society influenced the worldviews of Dietrich Bonhoeffer, Malcolm X, Aung San Suu Kyi, and other twentieth century mystic-activists. This enabled them to chart a course of response to injustice. Twenty-first-century mystic-activists also need an "apprenticeship" with mentors at the margins.

The Source of a Worldview from the Margins

The three primary mystic-activists in this book came to their marginal status by traveling three different paths. Their places in society influenced their perspectives and affected their journeys. Malcolm X's marginal viewpoint was the result of being born as a person of African descent in the United States. He said, "No, I'm not an American. I'm one of the 22 million black people who are the victims of Americanism.... And I see America through the eyes of the victim. I don't see any American dream; I see an American nightmare!"[3] Malcolm X had a "victim's eye view."[4]

Aung San Suu Kyi was born in Burma. Her father was a martyred hero who had fought for democracy against British colonialism. From her teens into adulthood, she lived outside of her home country. By the time she returned to Burma in her early forties, the country was under a military dictatorship. When she gave voice to her father's democratic sentiments, she discovered that the government no longer saw her as a member of the elite class. The government now viewed her as an outsider, while those at the margins embraced her as a leader.

Dietrich Bonhoeffer chose to sacrifice privilege to live in solidarity with persons at the margins. He gained a deep empathy for those who suffered and eventually an ability to see life through the eyes of those who faced injustice.

In his study of religious revolutionaries, Eugene Bianchi observed that leaders with a worldview from the margins can "rise up" from oppressed communities, such as Malcolm X. Others, such as Aung San Suu Kyi and Dietrich Bonhoeffer, "can link themselves" to movements against oppression "after spending a good portion of their lives as beneficiaries of the dominant culture."[5]

The authors of *Common Fire* identify two ways to understand the process of gaining a marginal perspective on life: "vulnerability-based marginality" and "values-based marginality."[6] Vulnerability-based marginality is when one's marginal perspective is the result of injustice or suffering experienced through no choice of one's own. People may inherit marginal status at birth, such as Malcolm X, or become vulnerable to it through social circumstances, as Aung San

Suu Kyi did. These individuals "transform the pain of their marginality into a deepened capacity for compassion and a strength of identity and purpose."[7] Values-based marginality involves the choice to embrace a marginal viewpoint because of one's ideals or, as is the case of mystic-activists, one's faith. Dietrich Bonhoeffer demonstrated a values-based marginality when he chose to act in solidarity with oppressed people because of his faith.

All social-justice activists can acquire a marginal worldview, whether they were born into it or not. This worldview offers mystic-activists a deeper analysis of oppression, a more authentic voice for social justice, and an opportunity for reconciliation.

Analyzing Oppression

Dietrich Bonhoeffer came to the conclusion that Nazi rule had to end if Jews in Germany were to survive. Without an insider's glimpse and a godly insight into the persecution of Jews in Germany, he might have accommodated the rule of Adolf Hitler, as many Christian religious leaders did. Bonhoeffer was better able to see injustice because he viewed the travesty of Nazi rule through the eyes of the Jewish population. He had gained the lens of the oppressed in the African American community of Harlem, New York. With this lens securely in place, the persecution of Jews in Germany became much clearer to him.

A worldview from the margins allows faith-inspired activists to better diagnose what creates and sustains oppressive social systems. Those who experience injustice often have the best insights into the character of oppression and what is needed to dismantle it. If they compare notes with other oppressed people about what injustice is and what its effects are, they may become experts on marginalization. Rigoberta Menchú believes that those at the margins are "the only ones capable of transforming society" because for them, "it's not just another theory."[8] Sometimes victims of injustice know what is required to create a just society but lack the power, influence, or resources to enact change.

Malcolm X "had an uncanny ability to diagnose the wounded psyche" of those who were oppressed.[9] He also pointed to the community of the victimized for insight. In a speech at Harvard he said:

> Whenever one is viewing this political system through the eyes of a victim, he sees something different. But today these twenty-two million black people who are victims of American democracy, whether you realize it or not, are viewing your democracy with new eyes. Yesterday our people used to look upon the American system as an American dream. But the black people today are beginning to realize that it is an American nightmare. What is a dream to you is a nightmare to us. What is hope to you has long since become hopeless to our people.[10]

Not only did Malcolm X use his own view to understand the problem, he used this perspective "to help others break with the paradigm of ruling-class thought" and understand "that the experience of exploitation and degradation at the hands of a racist system could be turned to a source of insight and emancipation."[11] The genius of Malcolm X's leadership "was that he gave back to his followers, in a more highly refined and clarified form, ideas and insights which in fact were rooted in their experiences."[12] The view from the margins offers mystic-activists wisdom regarding social change that can only be found in oppressed communities. Faith-inspired activists work to analyze this wisdom critically, refine it, and then give it voice.

An Authentic Voice for Justice

Marginalization also affirms the mystic-activist's authenticity—a hallmark of leadership that has "a kind of comfort with life at the edge."[13] Nowhere is authenticity more important than in the activist's denouncement of injustice and call for liberation. When Bonhoeffer married his faith to political understanding, he had to cry out against Nazism to remain authentic. Malcolm X's own experience of racism and his awareness of the plight of other African Americans gave his voice authenticity and the power to express his rage against racial injustice. In *Race Matters*, Cornel West notes, "Malcolm X articulated Black rage in a manner unprecedented in American history. His style of communicating this rage bespoke a boiling urgency and an audacious sincerity; the substance of what he said highlighted the chronic refusal of most Americans to acknowledge the sheer absurdity that confronts human beings of African descent in this country—the incessant assaults on Black intelligence, beauty, character, and possibility."[14]

Rage against injustice arises when one truly embraces the reality of marginalized people. Archbishop Oscar Romero of El Salvador began his leadership supporting the elite in his country. But during his country's civil war, like Bonhoeffer, his experience with the "outcast, the suspects, the maltreated, the powerless, the oppressed, the reviled" transformed his faith and his worldview.[15] Romero expressed a holy rage when he declared in a in a radio sermon on March 23, 1980, that the individual soldier had a higher moral authority than the oppressive government of El Salvador. He told soldiers to disobey orders that broke God's commandment not to kill. "In the name of God, then, in the name of this suffering people, whose cries rise to the heavens, every day more tumultuously, I ask you, I beg you, I order you in the name of God: stop the repression."[16] The following day, an assassin shot and killed Romero as he celebrated Eucharist. As is clear from the lives of Bonhoeffer, Malcolm X, Romero, and others, authenticity can be dangerous if those who represent power feel threatened by a mystic-activist's integrity.

Reconciliation Position

A marginal viewpoint places the mystic-activist in a position that can be used for reconciliation. A worldview blessed by marginality "makes it possible to hold several different perspectives and so gain a more complex and sensitive way of seeing, unavailable to those with only one point of view."[17] One who sees life clearly from the margins learns that there are many kinds of marginalization. Race, gender, class, age, ethnicity, sexual orientation, religion, and other social factors all frame oppression in different ways. Even more nuances appear when a person is marginalized in more than one way. Mystic-activists seek to understand the complex and multifaceted experience of life. Bonhoeffer's journey illustrates well his ability to embrace multiple viewpoints as he interpreted life from "the perspective of a black preacher in Harlem, of a French pacifist, of pastors concerned about political idolatry creeping into their churches, of a fellow minister with Jewish blood, of inmates at Nazi prisons and death camps, of conspirators torn between loyalty to country and conscience."[18]

Sociologist Charles V. Willie identifies this ability to view life through multiple lenses as a "principle of marginality." He defines marginal people as those "who live in, between, and beyond" the boundaries of race, culture, class, and the like.[19] Willie's principle of marginality expands beyond a view from below to a view from multiple perspectives—even the perspective of the oppressor, or a view from above.

Willie uses the biblical prophet Moses and Martin Luther King Jr. as illustrations. Both were born in marginal communities: Moses was a Hebrew enslaved in Egypt, and King was an African American in racist America. Yet both were educated in the ways of the dominant group: Moses was raised in Pharaoh's palace, and King was educated in graduate institutions that were predominantly white. Then, both found themselves leading movements to free their people. Moses led enslaved Hebrews out of Egypt. King worked to free his people from racial and economic bonds. King was killed while trying to liberate African American sanitation workers in Memphis, Tennessee.[20]

Cornel West calls people who operate in both the worlds of racial oppression and privilege "race-transcending prophets."[21] Race-transcending prophets are "people who never lose contact with their own particularity, yet refuse to be confined to it...enlarging rather than relinquishing their networks of belonging...they have come to a deeply held conviction that *everyone counts*."[22]

Learning to see from a privileged point of view is a powerful asset for mystic-activists. It enables them to gain access to ways of overcoming oppression. Rigoberta Menchú, whose mother tongue is Quiché, learned "the language of her oppressors in order to use it against them. For her, appropriating the Spanish language is an act which can change the course of history because it is the result of a decision: Spanish was a language which was forced upon her, but it has become a weapon in her struggle."[23]

Not only can a view from above help overthrow powerful oppression, it is also useful for the activist's own internal liberation. Martin Luther King Jr. identified this possibility: "Here is the true meaning and value of compassion and nonviolence when it helps us to see the enemy's point of view, to hear his questions, to know his assessment of ourselves. For from his view we may indeed see the basic weaknesses of our own condition, and if we are mature, we may learn and grow and profit from the wisdom of the brothers who are called the opposition."[24]

According to Willie, "Marginal people unite the clans, races and other groups in society and help them reconcile their differences" because they have "the ability to go beyond one's boundaries and see new patterns and possibilities."[25] This ability to see a world not confined by boundaries, full of new ways to organize, and fresh with possibilities for relating enables mystic-activists to work for reconciliation. Understanding the perspectives of those below and those above opens up alternatives not seen with a singular focus. To use less hierarchical language, to view life from both the center and the margins enriches the mystic-activist's ability to reconcile alienated communities.

Embracing a Worldview Immersed in the Margins

People whose identity society has denied may find it particularly difficult to see life through the lens of the oppressor or the privileged. And people from the dominant culture rarely choose to journey to the margins. Martin Luther King Jr. noted, "I guess I should have realized that few members of a race that has oppressed another race can understand or appreciate the deep groans and passionate yearnings of those that have been oppressed and still fewer have the vision to see that injustice must be rooted out by strong, persistent and determined action."[26]

Robert Kennedy asked for feedback from the margins in May of 1963, while serving as the attorney general of the United States.

He was raised in wealth and privilege with little awareness of poverty and racism. Yet President John F. Kennedy, Robert's brother, assigned him to interact with the Civil Rights Movement. Robert Kennedy invited noted social critic James Baldwin to assemble a group of African Americans to speak honestly to him about issues of race and poverty in the United States. A group that included sociologists, psychologists, activists, and artists met with Kennedy in New York City.

The meeting began with a polite exchange on the state of racism. Robert Kennedy made comments about the positive role of the government in matters of civil rights. Jerome Smith was a young civil rights activist in attendance who had been brutalized and arrested several times. Listening to the comments, he exploded. He said he wanted to vomit just being in the same room with Robert Kennedy who had done so little to support the freedom struggle of African Americans. Singer Lena Horne described what happened next. "This boy [Smith] just put it like it was. He communicated the plain, basic suffering of being a Negro. The primeval memory of everyone in the room went to work after that.... He took us back to the common dirt of our existence and rubbed our noses in it.... You could not encompass his anger, his fury, in a set of statistics."[27]

As Jerome Smith kept up his verbal assault of Kennedy, the attorney general turned away from Smith and ignored him. This made the others in the room even angrier, and they began to speak more bluntly too. Psychologist and educator Kenneth Clark recalled, "Bobby [Kennedy] became more silent and tense, and he sat immobile in the chair. He no longer continued to defend himself. He just sat, and you could see the tension and the pressure building in him." Clark reflected later that this was "the most intense, traumatic meeting in which I've ever taken part...the most unrestrained interchange among adults, head-to-head, no holds barred...the most dramatic experience I have ever had."[28] Kennedy biographer Konstantin Sidorenko sums up the meeting:

> It shook Robert Kennedy to the core of his beliefs.... It was the most important lesson any American public official had ever received on the anger and frustrations underlying segregation, poverty and the entire black experience. Most other prominent

men might have walked out of the room quickly. Robert Kennedy stayed there until the meeting fizzled out three hours after it began. He was angry, hurt and disgusted with the entire process. His reaction could have been that the entire issue was futile and a waste of time. Something very different happened. Bobby changed.[29]

Learning to understand life from those who are oppressed or suffering may be a painful, frightening affair. Transformation requires the sacrifice of assumptions and humility of spirit. Mystic-activists will never be effective in deep social change without stripping off condescension and expanding a one-dimensional viewpoint.

Finding God in the Margins

Oscar Romero did not begin his tenure as archbishop of El Salvador with a passion for the poor. Church officials, in collusion with state authorities, chose him because they believed he would not upset the status quo, in which a small group controlled most of their country's resources while the majority struggled for bare survival. As Romero met people in far-flung parishes, he saw their extreme poverty and the ruthless nature of the government. He also met with an unexpected encounter. Romero discovered the God he worshipped in the suffering poor of El Salvador. The archbishop fully awakened to this while officiating at the funeral of a priest friend whose parish was among the poor. As Romero celebrated Mass, he looked into the eyes of the gathered people and "he recognized God in the poor. The passion they were enduring was Christ's suffering in history." Romero knew intellectually that the church was more than the institution—more than "the hierarchy, Rome, theologians, or clerics." But it was finally in the midst of a funeral Mass that "he *experienced* God present in the people. Romero understood the poor as a sacrament of salvation. '*God needs the people themselves,*' he said, '*to save the world.*'"[30]

Oscar Romero's encounter with God in the marginalized poor themselves changed his understanding of the church. "The church, then, would betray its own love for God and its fidelity to the Gospel if it stopped being the 'voice for the voiceless,' a defender of the rights of the poor, a promoter of every just aspiration for liberation, a guide, an empowerer, a humanizer of every legitimate struggle to achieve a more just society, a society that prepares the way for the true kingdom of God in history."[31] Romero biographers Marie Dennis, Renny Golden, and Scott Wright ask, "Who else but God could be the source of such a change? How could a fifty-nine-year-old ecclesiastic at the pinnacle of church power, a man of circumspection, diplomacy, filial obedience, and orthodoxy, who enjoyed the esteem of Rome and his brother bishops, a man well received by the Salvadoran elite—how could such a man turn away from what seemed to be a well-established life path?" Their answer, "Only, it seems, by invitation of a God he had long before decided to follow, no matter what the cost."[32]

This encounter with God through marginalized people demonstrates the aptness of the designation *mystic-activists*. Faith-inspired activists cannot separate prayer from social justice. Liberation theologian Segundo Galilea observes, "The Other experienced in contemplative prayer is also experienced in the encounter with the others."[33]

Relating with People at the Margins

Oscar Romero discovered God through the people the El Salvadoran government exploited. This provided the spiritual foundation for his transformation. But it was through relationships with the people themselves and firsthand knowledge of their circumstances that Romero learned to see through their eyes. Rigoberta Menchú states, "I think that unless a religion springs from within the people themselves, it is a weapon of the system."[34] Dietrich Bonhoeffer spent time in Harlem with Union Seminary friend Frank Fisher and learned from the people there who lived daily with racism. Later, similar glimpses into the life of the Jewish community in Germany "provided him with a perspective few others either had or wanted [and] it meant more to him than it did for those he was seeking to help."[35]

We must not spiritualize or soften what it takes to engage people who live at the margins of a society. Dorothy Day was offended by the sights, sounds, and smells of poverty in New York City:

> The sight of homeless and workless men lounging on street corners or sleeping in doorways in broad sunlight appalled me. The sight of cheap lodging houses, dingy restaurants, the noise of subways and elevated railways, the clanging of streetcars jarred my senses. Above all the smell from the tenements, coming up from basements and areaways, from dank halls, horrified me. It is a smell like no other in the world and one never can become accustomed to it. I have lived with these smells now for many years, but they will always and ever affront me. I shall never cease to be indignant over the conditions which give rise to them.

Yet Day felt these same conditions strangely beckoned her to enter into a life of compassionate solidarity with the poor. "As I walked these streets back in 1917 I wanted to go and live among these surroundings; in some mysterious way I felt that I would never be freed from this burden of loneliness and sorrow unless I did."[36]

Malcolm X understood the margins because he was victimized by racism. Yet he knew that his experience needed to be validated and expanded by the witness of others. Malcolm X accomplished this by developing personal relationships with people at the grassroots by visiting "homes on Sunday afternoons, the traditional open-house time in the Black community. He held court around a meal with its aura of personal intimacy."[37]

Taking the Same Risks

The process of gaining a marginalized worldview begins as one feels the pulse of the divine beating at the core of oppressed communities. Then the mystic-activist spends time with people living in such settings. This commitment is tested. Will the person who chooses marginalization take the same risks that those trapped by injustice are required to take? Rigoberta Menchú said, in the context of the struggle for freedom in Guatemala, "We need leaders who are in danger, who run the same risks as the people."[38]

When mystic-activists take risks, this seals the relationship. Black liberation theologian James Cone writes regarding Bonhoeffer's radical theology: "What most white Protestant professors of theology overlook is that these are the words of a prisoner, a man who encountered the evils of Nazism and was killed in the encounter. Do whites really have the right to affirm God's death when they have actually enslaved men in God's name? It would seem that unless whites are willing to endure the pain of oppression, they cannot authentically speak of God."[39]

The military junta offers Aung San Suu Kyi a standing invitation to leave Burma at anytime. She can escape the challenges of the liberation struggle. Her decision to remain in Burma under house arrest is a choice to face the same risks as other people resisting the military junta.

Martin Luther King Jr. was noted for taking the same risks as those who followed his leadership. When he asked people to go to jail, he was often in the next cell. In the final days of his life, King increasingly took personal and political risks to challenge the structure of poverty, racism, and militarism.

Historian Vincent Harding talked with one of King's colleagues in the 1970s. He anonymously told Harding, "In a way, it was probably best for many of us who worked with Martin that he was killed when he was, because he was moving into some radical directions that very few of us had been prepared for." King's coworker continued, "And I don't think many of us on the staff would have been ready to take the risks of life, possessions, security, and status that such a move would have involved." Finally, the man told Harding, "I'm pretty sure I wouldn't have been willing."[40]

Mystic-activists never dismiss the consequences of taking risks, but as their lives become wedded to their vision, the risks seem less optional. The extent to which they no longer choose their risks reflects how much they have become one with the life of the oppressed.

Identifying with the Margins

Taking risks leads to solidarity with those at the margins. Malcolm X was born and raised among the oppressed. For him, identifying with those at the margins meant not leaving when he had the opportunity. Those born among the privileged can also connect with those at the margins. Dorothy Day took this connection to its limits: "When I first wrote of these experiences I wrote even more strongly of my identification with those around me. I was that mother whose child had been raped and slain. I was the mother who had borne the monster who had done it. I was even that monster, feeling in my own breast every abomination."[41] Oscar Romero summed it up, "It amounts to nothing more than the church's taking upon itself the lot of the poor."[42]

The worldview of mystic-activists becomes one with the perspectives of people at the margins in a deeply spiritual sense. Their thinking and action are immersed in realities external to their own world view. The Dalai Lama, the Tibetan Buddhist leader, writes that "when we enhance our sensitivity toward others' suffering through deliberately opening ourselves up to it, it is believed that we can gradually extend out compassion to the point where the individual feels so moved by even the subtlest suffering of others that they come to have an overwhelming sense of responsibility toward those others."[43]

As mystic-activists engage with people at the margins, they are drawn into a risk-filled commitment through the relationships they create. At some point there seems to be no way out. Their God, their friends, their passions, and their identity all are found at their new home on the margins of society.

What does it mean to embrace a worldview influenced by the margins? According to theologian John W. de Gruchy, for Bonhoeffer it meant

> ...solidarity with Jews who were being carted off to death camps. It meant proclaiming peace as his nation and others prepared for war. It meant raising disturbing questions, arising out of reflection on the gospel, within his church and among his students. It even meant praying for the defeat of his coun-

try, the Germany he loved so deeply. And it meant entering the shadowy world of the conspiracy, risking action on the boundaries of the church and Christian ethics in seeking to be faithful to Christ."

De Gruchy adds, "Finally it meant the hangman's noose."[44]

During the struggle against apartheid in South Africa, his native country, Allan Boesak was invited to speak at a conference on Bonhoeffer's theology. His questions echo those posed by the lives of mystic-activists.

> One must ask: "Can one be a theologian in South Africa or for that matter anywhere else, and not speak up for and not fight alongside the victims of oppression and tyranny?" Can one be a theologian and not find oneself compelled to be involved in the struggle for justice and for peace? Can one be a theologian and not be willing to place at risk all that one has, indeed, also one's life if necessary, in order to authenticate one's doing theology in the world?

Even though speaking of Bonhoeffer, Allan Boesak's conclusion rings true of the lives and worldviews of mystic-activists. "When I think of Bonhoeffer, I think of a theologian who has made it impossible since his life and death for anyone to do theology without understanding from the inside the meaning of struggle, the meaning of identification with those who are voiceless, the meaning of participating in the battles in this world that seek to establish justice and peace and humanity. Can one be a theologian and not do this?"[45]

Malcolm X, 1965
© Michael Ochs Archives/Corbis

5

MALCOLM X: "RECOGNIZING EVERY HUMAN BEING AS A HUMAN BEING"

In the final years of his life, Malcolm X adopted a new focus for his pursuit of freedom—human rights. Human rights took center stage in his message from the time he left the Nation of Islam in March 1964 until his murder in February 1965. He declared in a speech, "Human rights are something you were born with. Human rights are your God-given rights. Human rights are the rights that are recognized by all nations of this earth."[1]

A few days after this speech, Malcolm X left on a pilgrimage to Islam's holy city of Mecca. This visit accelerated the shift in his understanding of human relations. While in Mecca, Saudi Arabia, he described his experience with orthodox Islam: "They were *of all colors*, from blue-eyed blonds to black-skinned Africans... displaying a spirit of unity and brotherhood that my experiences in America had led me to believe could never exist between the white and the non-white."[2]

Malcolm X's spiritual transformation on pilgrimage caused a fundamental change in his outlook on reconciliation and social justice. He began experimenting with a new understanding of the human experience. He was moving beyond the limitations of a race-based approach for defining the human family. He stated in an interview a month before his death: "I believe in recognizing every human being as a human being, neither white, black, brown nor red. When you are dealing with humanity as one family, there's no question of integration or intermarriage. It's just one human being marrying another human being, or one human being living around another human being."[3] Malcolm X only came to this view in the final year of his life—a life spent battling dehumanization and exploitation and forging a human identity based in dignity, power, and respect.

Growing Up Malcolm Little

Malcolm Little was born on May 19, 1925, the fourth child of his parents (and seventh of his father, who had three children from a previous marriage). His society did not fully recognize his humanity because of the color of his skin, even before he was born. While Malcolm was in his mother's womb, Ku Klux Klan members surrounded his family's home in Omaha, Nebraska, terrorizing the Little family. This experience foreshadowed Malcolm's lifelong struggle against racism, which produced intense issues of identity. The attack resulted from the threat felt by racist whites, who thought his parents challenged the view that African Americans were inferior to whites. Earl and Louise Little were members of Marcus Garvey's Back-to-Africa movement—an effort that sought to instill pride in African Americans and make cultural connections to Africa, with the possibility of relocation to the continent. Through Garvey's organization, they sought "to embrace a black God, a black aim, and a black destiny."[4] The Littles lived in ways that intentionally challenged the status quo.

Life inside the Little household was often as tense as the turmoil outside. Earl Little was a strict disciplinarian, and he and Louise often fought. In addition to domestic stress, skin color played a role in the household. Earl and Louise Little were fighting for their rights as black people in a racist society, yet they also played out the psychologically damaging impact of color consciousness in their family dynamics. Malcolm felt that his father gave him preferential treatment because of his light complexion, while his mother considered him her least favorite child for the same reason. Earl was very dark skinned. Louise looked nearly white. In his autobiography Malcolm X wrote:

> My mother, who was born in Grenada, in the British West Indies, looked like a white woman. Her father *was* white. She had

straight black hair, and her accent did not sound like a Negro's. Of this white father of hers, I know nothing except her shame about it.... It was, of course, because of him that I got my reddish-brown 'mariny' color of skin, and my hair of the same color. I was the lightest child in our family.... I learned to hate every drop of that white rapist's blood that is in me.[5]

After Malcolm was born, the family eventually settled in Lansing, Michigan. Earl Little continued his work on behalf of the Marcus Garvey movement by preaching the Garvey message in local African American churches. A few years after moving to Michigan, the Littles purchased a house in an all white area. Malcolm was four years old. Shortly after moving into the house, Earl and Louise Little were informed that their deed contained a clause that said, "This land shall never be rented, leased, sold to, or occupied by...persons other than those of the Caucasian race."[6] Earl Little refused to leave his property. Their home was set on fire and burned to the ground. The police accused Earl Little of setting the fire himself. The family moved farther outside of the city. This time, their white neighbors hassled them and threw rocks at them, finally causing the Littles to move to a rural area.

When Malcolm was six, his father was found dead, run over by a streetcar. While the authorities called it an accident, some African Americans in Lansing wondered if whites had attacked Earl Little and placed him on the tracks in order to silence a man they considered an agitator.

After the death of her husband, Louise Little was left with seven children in a country in the midst of an economic depression. Malcolm's mother and the family encountered a seemingly uncaring state welfare system. Malcolm X remembered, "When the state Welfare people began coming to our house, we would come home from school sometimes and find them talking with our mother, asking a thousand questions. They acted and looked at her, and at us, and around in our house, in a way that had about it the feeling—at least for me—that we were not people. In their eyesight we were just *things*, that was all."[7]

The strain of raising seven children, economic troubles, and an ever-present racism slowly caused Louise Little to lose her vitality and emotional stability. When Malcolm was thirteen years old, his mother was committed to a state mental hospital, where she would remain for the next twenty-four years.

As Malcolm entered his teenage years, his parents were no longer a part of his life. The welfare system separated him from his siblings and placed him in a foster home as a dependent of the state. His placement with a white family served to increase his feeling of *otherness*. Malcolm described the dehumanizing experience with his foster parents, the Swerlins:

> They all liked my attitude, and it was out of their liking for me that I soon became accepted by them—as a mascot, I know now. They would talk about anything and everything with me standing right there hearing them, the same way people would talk freely in front of a pet canary. They would even talk about me, or about "niggers," as though I wasn't there, as if I wouldn't understand what the word meant. A hundred times a day, they used the word "nigger." I suppose that in their own minds, they meant no harm; in fact they probably meant well...I remember one day when Mr. Swerlin, as nice as he was, came in from Lansing, where he had been through the Negro section, and said to Mrs. Swerlin right in front of me, "I just can't see how those niggers can be so happy and be so poor." He talked about how they lived in shacks, but had those big shining cars out front. And Mrs. Swerlin said, me standing right there, "Niggers are just that way..." That scene always stayed with me...It was the same with the other white people, most of the local politicians, when they would come visiting the Swerlins. One of their favorite parlor topics was "niggers"...What I am trying to say is that it just never dawned on them that I could understand, that I wasn't a pet, but a human being. They didn't give me credit for having the same sensitivity, intellect, and understanding that they would have been ready and willing to recognize in a white boy in my position. But it has historically been the case with white people, in their regard for black people, that even though we might be *with* them, we weren't considered *of* them. Even though they appeared to have opened the door, it was still closed. Thus they never did really see *me*.[8]

Malcolm was often the only African American in his class at school. He was usually at or near the top of his class academically. In seventh grade, his class elected him class president. Malcolm wrote later reflecting on this occurrence, "It surprised me even more than other people. But I can see now why the class might have done it. My grades were among the highest in the school ... And I was proud; I'm not going to say I wasn't. In fact, by then, I didn't really have much feeling about being a Negro, because I was trying so hard, in every way I could, to be white."[9]

What Malcolm X described as the "first major turning point" of his life happened in the eighth grade. He was in the classroom with Mr. Ostrowski, his English teacher. Malcolm had received excellent grades in English class and believed that the teacher really liked him. Mr. Ostrowski asked Malcolm about his future plans, saying, "Malcolm, you ought to be thinking about a career. Have you been giving it thought?" Malcolm replied, "Well, yes, sir, I've been thinking I'd like to be a lawyer."

Mr. Ostrowski responded, "Malcolm, one of life's first needs is for us to be realistic. Don't misunderstand me, now. We all here like you, you know that. But you've got to be realistic about being a nigger. A lawyer—that's no realistic goal for a nigger. You need to think about something you *can* be. You're good with your hands—making things. Everybody admires your carpentry shop work. Why don't you plan on carpentry?"

Malcolm described how this made him feel:

> I was one of his top students, one of the school's top students—but all he could see for me was the kind of future "in your place" that almost all white people see for black people ... What made it really begin to disturb me was Mr. Ostrowski's advice to others in my class—all of them white ... They all reported that Mr. Ostrowski had encouraged what they had wanted. Yet nearly none of them had earned marks equal to mine. It was a surprising thing that I had never thought of it that way before, but I realized that whatever I wasn't, I *was* smarter than nearly all those white kids. But apparently I was still not intelligent enough, in their eyes, to become whatever *I* wanted to be.[10]

At age fifteen, Malcolm dropped out of school. He saw no purpose in continuing his education. Relentless racism marked Malcolm's life. Without the racial pride of his parents, he had no anchor to secure his identity in a sea of dehumanization. When Malcolm dropped out of school, he moved to the home of his older half sister Ella Collins in Boston, Massachusetts. After the death of Earl Little, she had reached out to her half siblings. Malcolm was impressed by the strength of her personality and her race pride: "She was the first really proud black woman I had ever seen in my life. She was plainly proud of her very dark skin. This was unheard of among Negroes in those days."[11] Collins hoped to direct her younger brother toward a more positive experience of his blackness through the thriving middle-class African American community in Boston. Malcolm X noted, "I didn't want to disappoint or upset Ella, but despite her advice, I began going down into the town ghetto section. That world of grocery stores, walk-up flats, cheap restaurants, poolrooms, bars, storefront churches, and pawnshops seemed to hold a natural lure for me."[12]

Malcolm spent the second half of his teen years becoming more and more involved in life on the streets of Boston and New York City as a hustler known as Detroit Red. He sold and used drugs. He directed men to prostitutes and he used women. Malcolm also burglarized homes, which eventually led to his arrest. He had internalized the racism that oppressed him, and he acted out this depersonalization in his choices.

Prison

The court sentenced Malcolm Little to ten years in prison, in February 1946. He was twenty years old and would serve six and a half years. He arrived in prison a bitter and belligerent man. His antisocial behavior during his first few years in prison often landed him in solitary confinement. He regularly expressed his dislike for religion, earning himself the nickname Satan.

While Malcolm X served time in prison, several of his siblings joined a small religious group called the Nation of Islam (NOI). The leader of the Nation of Islam, Elijah Muhammad taught that the NOI was the natural religion for persons of African descent and that whites were devils. This teaching appealed to Malcolm X and other African Americans because "the possibility that white people are Satan incarnate has the force not only of religious metaphor but of empirical truth—a hypothesis by which one can at least explain why one lives in a rat-ridden slum and works, if at all, carrying the white man's baggage and diapering the white man's babies."[13] Malcolm X converted to the Nation of Islam in the spring of 1948.

After his religious conversion, Malcolm X became a new man. He reshaped his life in preparation for a new vocation as a member of the Nation of Islam. He took greater advantage of the prison library to study a wide range of subjects: philosophy, history, world religions, mathematics, literature, etymology, science, the biographies of political leaders, African American history, and more. He wanted to support the teachings of the Nation of Islam using the "white man's" history. On the weekends, he would study up to fifteen hours a day. Malcolm X reflected in his autobiography, "I knew right there in prison that reading had changed forever the course of my life. As I see it today, the ability to read awoke inside me some long dormant craving to be mentally alive.... My homemade education gave me, with every additional book that I read, a little bit more sensitivity to the deafness, dumbness, and blindness that was afflicting the black race in America."[14]

In addition to his extensive study in prison, Malcolm X developed a skill that would become a hallmark of his leadership: public speaking. He joined the prison debate team. "But I will tell you that, right there, in the prison, debating, speaking to a crowd, was as exhilarating to me as the discovery of knowledge through reading had been."[15] Combining his strong debate skills with NOI teachings and the library studies that supported his new worldview, Malcolm X started to witness to other prisoners about his new faith. He described one such opportunity in his autobiography:

> I found that a lot of Negroes attended a Bible class, and I went there. Conducting the class was a tall, blond, blue-eyed (a perfect "devil") Harvard Seminary student... He had talked about Paul. I stood up and asked, "What color was Paul?" And I kept

talking, with pauses, "He had to be black...because he was a Hebrew...and the original Hebrews were black...weren't they?"... He said, "Yes." I wasn't through yet. "What color was Jesus...he was Hebrew, too...wasn't he?" Both the Negro and the white convicts had sat bolt upright. I don't care how tough the convict, be he brainwashed black Christian, or a "devil" white Christian, neither of them is ready to hear anybody saying Jesus wasn't white... He said, "Jesus was brown." I let him get away with that compromise. Exactly as I had known it would, almost overnight the Charlestown convicts, black and white, began buzzing with the story. Wherever I went, I could feel the nodding. And anytime I got a chance to exchange words with a black brother in stripes, I'd say, "My man! You ever heard about somebody named Elijah Muhammad?"[16]

By the time he left prison, Malcolm X had gained the necessary knowledge and skills to be a minister in the Nation of Islam. Malcolm X's friend Benjamin Karim writes, "Malcolm had made of prison a seminary."[17] Karim also notes that prison was Malcolm X's place of salvation:

> In prison, Malcolm told us, he found his salvation, because in prison he discovered Islam, which gave him a new life. Prison was Malcolm's cocoon. Inside it he reformed and educated himself. Malcolm shed one life form so a new one could be born. Malcolm called it his metamorphosis. Just as the caterpillar is transformed into a butterfly inside its cocoon, the drug peddler, street hustler, and larcenist emerged from prison as Malcolm X.[18]

Malcolm X wrote in a letter regarding his time in prison: "I was in prison before entering here... The solitude, the long moments of meditative contemplation, have given me the key to my freedom."[19] On August 7, 1952, he was released from prison.

Minister Malcolm X of the Nation of Islam

When Malcolm Little left prison he joined his family in Detroit. He found a job and entered the life of the Nation of Islam. His brothers were active as ministers. He soon received his "X" and officially became Malcolm X. The "X" replaced the slave master's name, symbolized the lost African family name, and anticipated a new God-given name in the future. This act was a powerful reclamation of a lost sense of humanity.

Elijah Muhammad recognized Malcolm X's passion for the faith and named him the assistant minister of the Detroit temple in June 1953. Soon he was sent to Boston to start a new temple. Next, he went to Philadelphia. Malcolm X was tireless in his work, expanding the ministry of the Nation of Islam. His success caused Elijah Muhammad to appoint the twenty-nine year old as the minister of Temple Number Seven in Harlem, New York City. Only one year after he had been selected as an associate minister in Detroit, Malcolm X began to oversee the Nation of Islam in the most important African American neighborhood in the largest city in the United States. He also continued launching new temples in other cities. Within three years of leaving prison, he took an organization of four hundred people with less than ten temples and tripled its size. By the time he left the NOI in 1964, he had started over two hundred new temples (later called "mosques" to stress their affinity to world Islam).

Malcolm X's success came, in part, because he was a skilled organizer. Perhaps even more important was that he knew his audience. The new members were poor and working-class African Americans from urban settings. Malcolm X had lived this life and he clearly understood "their disillusionment, fear, anger, cynicism, rage, unhappiness, isolation, poverty, and desperation, especially as it related to the pervasive and destructive force of white racism on their lives."[20] Later the Nation of Islam would attract black middle-class professionals who also recognized the impact of racism. Malcolm X was building a black African nation separate from whites. He was pursuing an agenda similar to his parent's passionate plans for the Garvey movement. He was reclaiming the human dignity of African American people.

The temple in Harlem gained increased attention and membership due to an incident in 1957. Two white policemen were breaking up an altercation on a street corner in Harlem. They instructed the people watching to keep moving. Two members of the Nation of Islam did not leave the scene but rather challenged the police officers on their abusive treatment of the suspect. One of the policemen grabbed Johnson X Hinton from behind and beat him with a nightstick. Then he was taken to the local precinct office. He had never been arrested before. The other NOI member called the leadership at the Harlem temple. Within thirty minutes, about fifty members of the Fruit of Islam (the NOI's security force) arrived at the police station and stood outside in formation. A crowd of local citizens also gathered.

Malcolm X arrived on the scene and entered the precinct building. He asked to see Hinton. At first the police refused to admit that he was there. Finally they acknowledged that Johnson X Hinton was there, but they would not allow Malcolm X to see him. So Malcolm X joined the Fruit of Islam on the street outside the station. By now the crowd had grown to nearly three thousand angry Harlem residents standing behind the disciplined members of the Fruit of Islam. It was after midnight and the police feared there might be a riot. So the police called in some of Harlem's respected leaders. One of them was James Hicks, a friend of Malcolm X and the editor of the *Amsterdam News*—Harlem's largest newspaper. He informed the police that Malcolm X was the only one in Harlem who could control the crowd.

So in the middle of the night, the deputy commissioner of the New York City Police Department met with Malcolm X in Hicks's office. The police commissioner asked Malcolm X to disperse the crowd. Malcolm X demanded first to see Johnson X Hinton to determine if he needed medical attention. The commissioner agreed. Malcolm X wrote, "When I saw our Brother Hinton, it was all I could do to contain myself. He was only semi-conscious. Blood had bathed his head and face and shoulders. I hope I never again have to withstand seeing another case of sheer police brutality like that."[21] An ambulance took Hinton to Harlem Hospital. Malcolm X and the Fruit of Islam walked to the hospital, followed by the crowd. Fearing the crowd, hospital officials gave Hinton back into the custody of the police immediately after he was treated. The police returned with Hinton to the police station.

As Malcolm X and the Fruit of Islam walked in formation the fifteen blocks down Lenox Avenue to Harlem Hospital and then back to the police station, more and more people joined this nighttime march until there were over five thousand people in the crowd. Upon his return to the precinct, Malcolm X agreed to disperse the crowd. He stepped out of the station, lifted his arm, and signaled to the crowd. According to James Hicks, "It was eerie, because these people just faded into the night. It was the most orderly movement of four thousand to five thousand people I've ever seen in my life—they just simply disappeared—right before our eyes."[22] Hicks heard the police commissioner say, "This is too much power for one man to have." Hicks interpreted his statement to mean that it was too much power for one black man to have.[23]

The membership of the Nation of Islam in Harlem grew from a few hundred to more than two thousand after the Johnson X Hinton episode. Benjamin Karim reflected later on the deputy commissioner's comment that no one (black) should have that much power.

> It was that same power and presence which so impressed and frightened the police that also attracted me and thousands of young so-called Negroes to Malcolm. Here was a man who could walk boldly into the jaws of the lion, walk proud and tall into the territory of the enemy, the station house of the 28th Precinct, and force the enemy to capitulate. Here was a man who could help restore the heritage, the pride of race and pride of self, that had been carefully stripped from us over the four hundred years of our enslavement here in White America.[24]

The relationship between Malcolm X and his leader, the Honorable Elijah Muhammad—the Messenger of Allah, was like that of a father and a son. Elijah Muhammad promoted Malcolm X to national spokesman, the person who would represent the leader when needed. One of Malcolm X's friends described an episode that exemplified their relationship: "I sat in Elijah Muhammad's home one Saturday morning while he was lecturing a group of ministers. The doorbell rang, and a servant came in and announced that

Malcolm had come. Elijah's eyes lit up as if the prodigal son was home. He leaped up from his seat, and when Malcolm appeared they embraced and kissed. Seeing this could not have left room to doubt their affection for each other."[25] In 1958, Malcolm X asked for Elijah Muhammad's blessing to marry Sister Betty X. Later, he named one of his daughters after the Messenger using the Arabic feminine form of Elijah, "Ilyasah."

Elijah Muhammad's message was central to Malcolm X's preaching and teaching. Malcolm X sought to restore to African Americans their sense of humanity. He did this through telling the NOI's truth about the white man and highlighting blacks' cultural connection to Africa. He articulated the simmering rage of African Americans about racism.

Malcolm X also wanted African Americans to learn to love themselves as blacks. He felt that a chief impediment to this goal was that many African Americans accepted that the norm of humanity was whiteness. Therefore too many African Americans were striving to be like whites—whether they were conscious of this or not. Regarding what he considered blacks' inordinate love for whites he said, "It is not possible for you to love a man whose chief purpose in life is to humiliate you and still be considered a normal human being."[26] In a message at Abyssinian Baptist Church in Harlem (the same congregation that Bonhoeffer had attended) he declared:

> How can anybody ask us do we hate the man who kidnapped us four hundred years ago, brought us here and stripped us of our history, stripped us of our culture, stripped us of our language, stripped us of everything you could use today to prove that you were ever part of the human family, brought you down to the level of an animal, sold you from plantation to plantation like a sack of wheat, sold you like a sack of potatoes, sold you like a horse and a cow, and then hung you up from one end of the country to the other, and then you ask me do I hate him? Why, your question is worthless![27]

When civil rights activist Stokely Carmichael (who later took the name Kwame Ture) was a student at Howard University, he and other students organized a debate between Malcolm X and Bayard

Rustin. Rustin was a mainstream civil rights leader and organizer of the March on Washington in 1963, where Martin Luther King Jr. gave his "I Have a Dream" speech. The subject of the debate was "Integration or Separation?" Malcolm X joined the student organizers prior to the public event. Carmichael's initial impression was one of awe:

> There he stood, smiling almost diffidently in the doorway. Tall, slender, his horn-rimmed glasses glinting, the expression of his lean face alert, carrying himself erect, with a formality, a quiet dignity, in his posture, yet beneath it an unmistakable warmth. Without doing a thing for a moment he simply commanded the entire space.... Malcolm had a *presence*, something you could not miss but neither could you quite name.... He was unfailingly courteous, treating each questioner and his or her question with wit, care, and a great respect, which put everyone at ease...only somewhat at ease, not entirely. Because at the same time he always radiated a ripple of tension, a banked power, and a quality of alert, guarded watchfulness that really was like a cat's. And everyone present could feel it.[28]

Malcolm X always won his debates. And this was no exception. His prison practice had equipped him well. Rustin was one of the few civil rights leaders willing to debate Malcolm X. Martin Luther King Jr. never accepted the invitation. Malcolm X's message that day focused on his notion that the real issue was not integration or separation but rather "respect and recognition as human beings" for the twenty-two million African Americans in the United States.[29] Stokely Carmichael described what happened that helped restore the human self worth of the African American students gathered that night:

> What Malcolm demonstrated that night in Crampton Auditorium on the Howard campus was the raw power, the visceral potency, of the grip our unarticulated collective blackness held over us. I'll never forget it. A spotlight picked him out as he strode, slim, erect, immaculately tailored, to the mike on an otherwise darkened stage. When he uttered the traditional Islamic greeting of peace, *salaam aleikum*, the answer came roar-

ing back at him from the center of the hall. "*Wa aleikum as salaam*".... Then Malcolm went into his introduction of himself. I think I remember it exactly after thirty-five years. It was classic theological nationalism. "*Salaam aleikum*. I come to you in the name of all that is eternal"—pause—"the black man." This time, the deep roar came from all over the hall, and it was visceral. "Before you were American, you were black." Roar. "Before you were Republican...you were black." Roar. "Before you were Democrat...you were black." Biggest roar. After each variation a roar of affirmation. The hairs tingled on the nape of my neck. The audience just erupted around me, I mean *erupted*. It seemed entirely spontaneous, a sound somewhere between a howl and a roar. As if this gathering of young Africans—from the continent, the Caribbean, America—were freed to recognize their oneness, to give loud affirmation to something they were being educated, conditioned really, to suppress and deny: our collective blackness.[30]

Leaving the Nation of Islam

In April 1962, the Los Angeles police killed Ronald X Stokes, the secretary of the Nation of Islam in that city, and brutalized many others in an unprovoked raid of the NOI mosque by seventy-five police officers. Malcolm X had established this mosque and had known Stokes quite well. Elijah Muhammad sent him to investigate the matter and organize the funeral. Nine days after the event, Stokes's murder was declared a justifiable homicide. Malcolm X and other ministers of the Nation of Islam began to contemplate some form of retaliation against the police. Elijah Muhammad overruled this saying that Allah would bring vengeance.

This disagreement between Malcolm X and his leader reflected Malcolm X's growing frustration with the Nation of Islam's practice of talking tough but taking no action. "You know, we talk about people being bitten by dogs and mowed down by fire hoses, we talk about our people being brutalized in the civil rights movement, and we haven't done anything to help them. We haven't done anything. And now we've had one of our own brothers killed and we still haven't done anything."³¹ Malcolm X wanted the Nation of Islam to engage in the political arena. Elijah Muhammad only envisioned the NOI as a religious group confined to religious aspirations. Malcolm X hoped for more than just change in individuals brought about by religion. He desired revolution in society, and his "fanatic commitment to the liberation of the black poor alienated him not only from most whites and many persons in the black middle class, but also, as it turned out, from his own religious community and from Elijah Muhammad as well."³²

The lack of action or political involvement was not the only factor in his growing frustration with the Nation of Islam. Malcolm X also hungered for a closer relationship with worldwide Islam. International students from Islamic communities would approach him after a speech.

> My white-indicting statements notwithstanding, they felt that I was sincere in considering myself a Muslim—and they felt if I was exposed to what they always called "true Islam," I would "understand it, and embrace it." Automatically, as a follower of Elijah Muhammad, I had bridled whenever this was said. But in the privacy of my own thoughts after several of these experiences, I did question myself: if one was sincere in professing a religion, why should he balk at broadening his knowledge of that religion?³³

Elijah Muhammad's son Wallace had studied Arabic and the Qur'an. He recognized that the theology of the Nation of Islam was not consistent with that of orthodox Islam. Wallace shared his concerns and knowledge with Malcolm.

Malcolm X began to change the way he presented his message. On a television interview show in March 1963, a reporter asked what it meant to be a Muslim. Malcolm X answered, "One becomes a Muslim only by accepting the religion of Islam, which means belief in one God, Allah. Christians call him Christ, Jews call him Jehovah. Many people have many different names but he is the creator of the universe."[34] He also spoke about the practices of Muslims in ways that mirrored the practices of Islamic people around the world. This was quite a departure from his normal fare of presenting his faith in terms of black separation and the exalted status of Elijah Muhammad as one who had seen Allah in human flesh. Another factor in Malcolm's interest in traditional Islam was that his half sister Ella had converted to Sunni Islam, the main branch of Islam, in the late 1950s. Also Malcolm X traveled to Mecca in 1959, and secured an authorized English translation of the Holy Qur'an which he studied regularly.

Malcolm X's growing dissatisfaction with the Nation of Islam would more than likely have led him to attempt to reform the NOI from within. But the discovery of immorality in the life of his religious leader, father figure, and mentor led to his departure from the NOI. Malcolm X learned that Elijah Muhammad had engaged in a series of extramarital affairs with his young secretaries and had fathered several children by these unions. The leader of a religion that forbade sex outside of marriage and excommunicated those who had committed such offenses was guilty of this same immoral behavior. Malcolm X described the impact of these revelations: "My faith had been shaken in a way that I can never fully describe. For I had discovered Muslims had been betrayed by Elijah Muhammad himself."[35]

Malcolm X spoke to Elijah Muhammad about his adultery and even proposed that the Messenger was fulfilling prophecy in these actions. "I actually had believed that if Mr. Muhammad was not God, then he surely stood next to God. What began to break my faith was that, try as I might, I couldn't hide, I couldn't evade, that Mr. Muhammad, instead of facing what he had done before his followers, as human weakness or as fulfillment of prophecy … Mr. Muhammad had, instead, been willing to hide, to cover up what he had done." Malcolm X reflected, "I had believed in Mr. Muhammad more than he believed in himself. And that was how, after twelve years of never thinking for as much as five minutes about myself, I became able finally to muster the nerve, and the strength, to start facing the facts, to think for myself."[36] Malcolm X's wife Betty Shabazz said that her husband told her, "The foundation of my life seems to be coming apart."[37] His older brother Wilfred Little, also a minister in the NOI, noted, "All the wind was taken out of his sails when he realized what the Messenger had done."[38]

Malcolm X did not immediately leave the Nation of Islam after learning of Elijah Muhammad's cover-up of his adultery. He struggled to stay in an organization that had profoundly changed his life and the lives of many others. His disappointment with his leader, as well as his desire to move closer to traditional Islam and to engage with the civil rights movement, were not the only factors affecting his standing in the Nation of Islam. Malcolm X's popularity and influence threatened Elijah Muhammad's inner circle of leaders and family members at the NOI headquarters in Chicago. Their jealousy led them to sabotage Malcolm X's credibility with the Messenger and to plan for his demotion if not ouster. The leaders were also looking out for their own future.

Malcolm X provided them with an opportunity in a speech he gave after President John Kennedy's assassination in November 1963. Elijah Muhammad told him to make no comments on the president's death. Kennedy was popular with African Americans and Muhammad did not want any bad press for the NOI. In a question-and-answer session following his speech, Malcolm X responded to a question about the death of Kennedy. Using an illustration from farming, Malcolm said that, given the involvement of the United States in the assassinations of other world leaders, Kennedy's assassination was a case of the chickens coming home to roost. This remark gained national attention. In response, Elijah Muhammad suspended Malcolm X for ninety days. Soon, the ninety-day suspension was extended indefinitely. Clearly, Malcolm X was no longer welcome in the organization he helped build.

Malcolm X's departure from the Nation of Islam was probably inevitable given the reasons noted above, and it came in March 1964. His new freedom caused Malcolm X to appear like "a man coming out of a lightless cellar and blinking at the day."[39] Malcolm X himself said, "I feel like a man who has been asleep somewhat and under someone else's control. I feel what I'm thinking and saying now is for myself. Before, it was for and by the guidance of Elijah Muhammad. Now I think with my own mind."[40] Malcolm X embraced an agenda much broader than that of the Nation of Islam and became an agent for change in the entire African American community—not just as a minister of the Nation of Islam. The break with the NOI gave him time to reflect on how he had changed and the freedom to embrace a new path. His last fifty weeks of life were to be his most creative.

Joining World Islam

On March 8, 1964, Malcolm X announced that he was leaving the Nation of Islam and launching a new mosque in New York City called the Muslim Mosque, Inc. "This gives us a religious base and the spiritual force necessary to rid our people of the vices that destroy the moral fiber of our community.... The Muslim Mosque, Inc., will remain wide open for ideas and financial aid from all quarters. Whites can help us, but they can't join us. There can be no Black-white unity until there is first some Black unity."[41] The launch of a new mosque "more closely linked him to the Muslim world. Establishing links with Sunni Islam invariably meant that he had to become more global in his approach to matters of race, religion, and politics."[42]

In April 1964, Malcolm X traveled to Mecca to make the hajj, the pilgrimage required of all Muslims who are physically and economically able to make it. This act sealed his relationship with traditional Islam and gave him credibility as a Muslim leader. The pilgrimage was also a time of personal conversion. It offered him the opportunity to embrace the fullness of his own humanity. "In my thirty-nine years on this earth, the Holy City of Mecca had been the first time I had ever stood before the Creator of All and felt like a complete human being."[43] His vision for his life's work was also refocused. "I'm for truth, no matter who tells it. I'm for justice, no matter who it is for or against. I'm a human being first and foremost, and as such I'm for whoever and whatever benefits humanity *as a whole*."[44]

Malcolm X's embrace of orthodox Sunni Islam allowed him to accept his own sense of self without dismissing the humanity of others. The pilgrimage showed him that whites were not inherently evil racists—and this permitted him to accept the full humanity of whites. They were not born devils. This first struck him on his way to Mecca, surrounded by Muslims of all races, including whites.

> Packed in the plane were white, black, brown, red, and yellow people, blue eyes and blond hair, and my kinky red hair—all together, brothers! All honoring the same God Allah, all in turn giving equal honor to each other.... In America, "white man" meant specific attitudes and actions toward the black man, and toward all other non-white men. But in the Muslim world, I had seen that men with white complexions were more genuinely brotherly than anyone else had ever been. That morning was the start of a radical alteration in my whole outlook about "white" men.[45]

The Mecca journey radically changed Malcolm X's understanding of humanity. "My pilgrimage broadened my scope. It blessed me with a new insight. In two weeks in the Holy Land, I saw what I never had seen in thirty-nine years here in America. I saw all *races*, all *colors*—blue-eyed blonds to black-skinned Africans—in *true* brotherhood! In unity! Living as one! Worshiping as one!... The true Islam has shown me that a blanket indictment of all white people is as wrong as when whites make blanket indictments against blacks."[46]

Malcolm X became inclusive concerning race and religion. He made speeches around Harlem and elsewhere proclaiming, "True Islam taught me that it takes *all* of the religious, political, economic, psychological, and racial ingredients, or characteristics, to make the Human Family and the Human Society complete." He declared that even his understanding of friendship had changed. "Since I learned the *truth* in Mecca, my dearest friends have come to include *all* kinds—some Christians, Jews, Buddhists, Hindus, agnostics, and even atheists! I have friends who are called capitalists, Socialists, and Communists! Some of my friends are moderates, conservatives, extremists—some are even Uncle Toms! My friends today are black, brown, red, yellow, and *white!*"[47]

The pilgrimage to Mecca was also part of Malcolm X's overall strategy to prepare for ministry in orthodox Islam. He was "undertaking a rigorous program of preparation and examination under the aegis of the leading religious figures of the Muslim world." This education continued until October 1964, when Malcolm X went to Egypt for "a final examination before the rector of Cairo's Al-Azhar University." This process "provided Malcolm with credentials as a religious teacher charged with 'the duty to propagate Islam and offer every available assistance and facilities to those who wish conversion.'"[48]

When Malcolm X returned to the United States, following his conversion in Mecca and his changed view of whites, he was asked if he would start calling himself by his Muslim Arabic name, El-Hajj Malik El-Shabazz. He replied, "I'll continue to use Malcolm X as long as the situation that produced it exists. Going to Mecca was the solution to my personal problem; but it doesn't solve the problem for my people."[49] Malcolm X never changed his mind that "white American *society* was deeply and perhaps irretrievably racist—that our past and present together had so poisoned all of us, black and white, that we could not even look at one another independently of color and all that color meant between us. Mecca remained one thing for him, America another."[50]

Reaching Out to Build New Partnerships

After the pilgrimage to Mecca, Malcolm X visited several African countries. What Mecca provided spiritually, the African continent provided culturally and politically. Mecca offered his soul a homecoming. Africa gave his African identity "the emotional bath of the homecoming."[51] In Nigeria, a student organization gave him the name Omowale, which means "the child has come home" in the Yoruba language. Malcolm X had previously exclaimed to students in Ghana, "I don't feel that I am a visitor in Ghana or in any part of Africa. I feel that I am home."[52] Malcolm X was on the African continent nearly half of his last year of life.

Upon his return from Mecca and visits to several African countries, Malcolm X launched a second organization, the Organization of Afro-American Unity (OAAU). Whereas Muslim Mosque, Inc., was a religious organization, the OAAU provided a vehicle for organizing that did not require members to become Muslims. Malcolm X declared at the founding of the OAAU, "We declare our right on this earth to be a man, to be respected as a human being, to be given the rights of a human being in this society, on this earth, in this day, which we intend to bring into existence by any means necessary."[53]

Malcolm X focused on recruiting three groups to carry out his vision for the OAAU. The first group was "composed of progressive segments of the Black middle-class and working-class activists in Harlem united around a community-based agenda of and struggle against the common forms of ghetto exploitation." The work for unity among Harlem blacks was an outgrowth of Malcolm X's years as a minister of the Nation of Islam in New York City. The second group was the result of his trips overseas to engage "allies in Africa and the Third World who could get international recognition for his organization." Finally he sought to build bridges to leaders "in the Civil Rights movement who supported Malcolm's desire for reconciliation." Through reaching out to African American students in the Civil Rights movement he also gained "access to the radicalized White students."[54]

The partnerships with leaders in Africa were quite successful as a result of his trips there in his last year of life. These African alliances led to Malcolm X's plan to present a petition in the United Nations that charged the United States with violating the human rights of its African American citizens. This was similar to petitions that had been debated in the United Nations regarding South Africa and Rhodesia (now Zimbabwe), both ruled by white supremacist governments. Many African leaders were supportive when he introduced the petition at a meeting of the Organization of African Unity (upon which Malcolm X had modeled the OAAU).

Malcolm X's vision included movements for social change and human rights throughout the world. He recognized similarities in liberation struggles in Africa, Asia, and Latin America with civil rights movements in the United States.

Malcolm X's goal of better relationships with the civil rights leaders in the United States required humility on his part. He had been a harsh critic of the Civil Rights Movement and its commitment to nonviolence. But he reached out and asked to be given a second chance at relationship, noting that he was a different person, independent of the Nation of Islam and post-Mecca.

Most civil rights leaders welcomed Malcolm's entreaties, including Martin Luther King Jr. A few weeks after Malcolm X announced his independence from the NOI, he and King were both in the visitor's gallery of the United States Senate building for the debate on the Civil Rights Act of 1964. After the session, they spoke to each other and were interviewed jointly by a reporter who just happened to see them standing next to each other.[55] King made contact with Malcolm X through his lawyer, Clarence Jones, suggesting the two meet to discuss the petition Malcolm X planned to present to the United Nations. A meeting was scheduled but did not occur.[56] The two did speak to each other several times by phone.

On February 4, 1965, Malcolm X spoke in Selma, Alabama, at the invitation of the Student Nonviolent Coordinating Committee (SNCC). SNCC and King's organization, the Southern Christian Leadership Conference, were actively leading a protest campaign for voting rights in Selma. King was in jail at the time. Malcolm X did confer privately with Coretta Scott King, Martin's wife, after he spoke.

Malcolm X and Martin Luther King Jr. spoke by phone on February 14. According to William Kunstler, a lawyer who served both Malcolm X and King, "There was sort of an agreement that they would meet in the future and work out a common strategy, not merge their two organizations—Malcolm then had the Organization of Afro-American Unity and Martin, of course, was the president of the Southern Christian Leadership Conference—but that they would work out a method to work together in some way."[57] Malcolm X's home was fire bombed later that night. And two days before a scheduled meeting with King, Malcolm X was assassinated.[58]

Malcolm X was also seeking to build broader alliances with whites. He began proclaiming a more inclusive view of whites. "You will find that [Blacks and whites] will eventually meet down the road.... So we're not against people because they're white. But we're against those who practice racism."[59] Speaking in England to students at Oxford University he declared: "In my opinion the young generation of whites, Blacks, browns, whatever else there is—you're living at a time of extremism, a time of revolution, a time when there's got to be a change...and a better world has to be built, and the only way it's going to be built is with extreme methods. And I for one will join in with anyone, I don't care what color you are, as long as you want to change this miserable condition that exists on this earth."[60]

Malcolm X had not been as charitable toward white students during his days in the Nation of Islam. A young woman from a New England college booked a flight to New York after Malcolm X spoke at her college. She went to the Nation of Islam's restaurant in Harlem looking for Malcolm X. He recorded their meeting:

> I just happened to be there when she came in. Her clothes, her carriage, her accent, all showed Deep South white breeding and money. At that college, I told how the antebellum white slavemaster even devilishly manipulated his own woman. He convinced her that she was "too pure" for his base "animal instincts." With this "noble" ruse, he conned his own wife to look away from his obvious preference for the "animal" black woman. So the "delicate mistress" sat and watched the plantation's little mongrel-complexioned children, sired obviously by her father, her husband, her brothers, her sons. I said at that college that the guilt of American whites included their knowledge that in hating Negroes, they were hating, they were rejecting, they were denying, their own blood. Anyway, I'd never seen anyone I ever spoke to before more affected than this little white college girl.[61]

After finding Malcolm X, the young woman asked, "Don't you believe there are any *good* white people?"

He replied, "People's *deeds* I believe in, Miss—not their words."

She asked, "What can I *do*?"

Malcolm X responded, "Nothing."

The woman left the restaurant crying.[62]

Malcolm X reflected on that incident in the light of his new point of view toward whites and said: "I regret that I told her that. I wish now that I knew her name, or where I could telephone her, or write to her, and tell her what I tell white people now when they present themselves as being sincere, and ask me, one way or another, the same thing that she asked.... In many parts of the African continent I saw white students helping Black people. Something like this kills a lot of argument."[63]

Malcolm X's Last Days

Malcolm X did not live long enough to fully spell out his vision or to see it realized in concrete form. "I can capsulize how I feel—I'm for the freedom of the 22 million Afro-Americans by any means necessary. *By any means necessary.* I'm for a society in which our people are recognized and respected as human beings, and I believe that we have the right to resort to *any means necessary* to bring that about. So when you ask me where I'm headed, what can I say? I'm headed in any direction that will bring us some immediate results."[64]

The last few weeks of Malcolm X's life were stressful. He was under intense surveillance from local, national, and international governmental agencies. He received regular death threats from members of the Nation of Islam because he stated publicly that their theology was bad and their leader was an adulterer. On February 14, his house was set on fire by Molotov cocktails as he, his wife Betty (four months pregnant with twin girls), and their four daughters were sleeping. Malcolm X was nearly bankrupt. He tried to obtain life insurance to protect his family in case he was murdered. He was denied. On February 20, Malcolm called a business meeting of the OAAU, at which he said: "I don't care about myself. I only want to protect my family and the OAAU. No matter what happens to me personally, it is important that the OAAU continues to exist, do you understand that?... I never expected to die of old age. I know the power structure will not let me. I know that I have done the very best that I could to help our people."[65]

Malcolm X was scheduled to speak at an OAAU rally at the Audubon Grand Ballroom in Harlem on Sunday afternoon, February 21, 1965. He arrived about three o'clock. Malcolm X had called his wife, Betty, earlier and asked that she and the children come for the rally. Just before he went out into the ballroom to speak, Malcolm X said to one of his colleagues, "I just don't *feel* right."[66] After he greeted the audience, three men near the platform shot Malcolm

X as his family and friends watched. Malcolm X died shortly after being shot.

Prince Mohmaed Al-Faysal of Saudi Arabia had met Malcolm X on his pilgrimage to Mecca. He said of Malcolm X's death: "I think he was a great loss, especially to America. Because here is a man who has, in spite of his starting as a racist, sectarian person, developed into a force of reconciliation. And had he been given a chance, Malcolm would have changed American society, more than anybody else in recent history."[67] Malcolm X wrote in his autobiography:

> Sometimes, I have dared to dream to myself that one day, history may even say that my voice—which disturbed the white man's smugness, and his arrogance, and his complacency—that my voice helped to save America from a grave, possibly even a fatal catastrophe.... And if I can die having brought any light, having exposed any meaningful truth that will help destroy the racist cancer that is malignant in the body of America—then, all of the credit is due to Allah.[68]

6

AN IDENTITY ROOTED IN HUMANITY

Malcolm X's message, ministry, and even more, his identity, went through a rapid metamorphosis during the final year of his life. He cast aside a black separatism that had defined his work and his person for many years. Emerging in its place was an awareness that we share a common humanity. Malcolm X stated in a speech at Dartmouth College in the month before he died, "We must approach the problem as humans first, and whatever else we are second.... It is a situation which involves humans not nationalities. It is in this frame of reference that we must work."[1] Malcolm X's faith propelled him forward toward this new view. His embrace of orthodox Islam and his pilgrimage to Mecca transformed his identity. He said that it was in Mecca that he first felt like a human being. In a stunning reversal, his identity was no longer anchored in his blackness—though he never lost his racial pride. Rather, his identity was rooted in his humanity.

Malcolm X was also redefining the cause he had fought so hard for—the liberation of African American people—in terms of human rights. In one of his final speeches, Malcolm X declared, "The Black man in the Western Hemisphere, especially in the United States, is beginning to see where his problem is not one of civil rights, but it is rather one of human rights. And that in the human rights context it becomes an international issue. It ceases to be a Negro problem, it ceases to be an American problem. It becomes a human problem, a problem of human rights, a problem of humanity, a problem for the world."[2]

A belief in our common humanity is critical for mystic-activists trying to make sense of the inhumane nature of injustice and oppression throughout the world. Malcolm X's life offers a glimpse into the dehumanization of oppression and the hopeful process of rediscovering one's essence as a human being. Faith-inspired activists go through an identity defining process as they develop their leadership.

Defining Human Identity

Mohandas Gandhi once said, "We are all, first and foremost, human beings and we must relate to one another on that naked basis."[3] We must first arrive at an understanding of what it means to be human in order to understand the significance of defining one's own identity and the identity of others as human. The process of identifying the fundamental nature of humanity is fraught with challenges. Its troublesome history, more often than not, has resulted in depersonalization. When Christian missionaries arrived in the Americas, for instance, many who thought their efforts defended the humanity of indigenous people actually contributed to the dehumanization of the original Americans. Theologian George Tinker notes, "They failed to notice, let alone acknowledge, our personhood. They saw our cultures and our social structures as inadequate and needing to be replaced with what they called 'christian civilization.' Even as they argued liberally for the humanity of Indian people, they denied our personhood."[4]

While acknowledging the problematic nature of this endeavor, I still attempt to discover an understanding of humanity that can guide this discussion of mystic-activists—even if the definition is tentative. In some faith traditions, to be human is to be created in the image of God. From her tradition, Aung San Suu Kyi notes, "As a Buddhist, if you really want to consider what we, as human beings, are here for it's quite simple: we are trying to achieve enlightenment and to use the wisdom that is gained to serve others, so that they too might be free from suffering. While we can't all be Buddhas, I feel a responsibility to do as much as I can to realize the enlightenment to the degree that I can, and to use it to relieve the suffering of others."[5]

Theologian and social critic Howard Thurman regularly contemplated the meaning of humanity as he sought to address issues of racism in the United States. Thurman pondered deeply and wrote extensively on the subject a generation prior to Malcolm X's conclusion that the issue facing African Americans was really a human issue. Thurman's insights guide my attempt to gain clarity about what it means for mystic-activists to embrace a common humanity.

Thurman began with the concern that "the burden of being black and the burden of being white is so heavy that it is rare in our society to experience oneself as a human being." Then he posed the question, "Precisely what does it mean to experience oneself as a human being?" He came to believe that "the individual must have a sense of kinship to life that transcends and goes beyond the immediate kinship of family or the organic kinship that binds him ethnically or 'racially' or nationally.... He sees himself as a part of a continuing, breathing, living existence. To be a human being, then, is to be essentially alive in a living world."[6] Thurman contended that people experience their humanness when they are not "male or female, yellow or green or black or white or brown, educated or illiterate, rich or poor, sick or well, righteous or unrighteous—but a naked human spirit that spills over into other human spirits as they spill over into [us]."[7] Individuals are most fully aware of their human identity when exclusive and distinctive identifiers recede to secondary importance.

People recognize their humanity when they experience themselves "as being of infinite worth."[8] Malcolm X believed that self-worth was a source of human identity. "Our objective is complete freedom, complete justice, complete equality, by any means necessary. That never changes. Complete and immediate recognition and respect as human beings, that doesn't change, that's what all of us want. I don't care what you belong to—you still want that, recognition and respect as a human being."[9] When identity rests on feeling superior to another, or more valuable than someone else, it is a false sense of humanity.

Howard Thurman believed that when people embrace their worth they "can hear the sound of the genuine in other human beings." Faith-inspired activists need to accept their own self-worth and encourage a similar process in others if a just community is ever to emerge. Thurman stated, "One man's response to the sound of the genuine in another man is to ascribe to the other man the same sense of infinite worth that one holds for oneself."[10] In his final days, Malcolm X articulated a similar perspective, "I believe in recognizing every human being as a human being, neither white, black, brown nor red. When you are dealing with humanity as one family, there's no question of integration or intermarriage. It's just one human being marrying another human being, or one human being living around and with another human being."[11] To root one's identity in humanity is to experience a sense of aliveness free from particular identifiers, to embrace one's own worth and the equal worth of others, and to recognize a transcendent aspect to the whole adventure.

The Dehumanization of Identity

People are born fully human. Immediately after birth, one's "identity formation" begins through a social process involving an assortment of factors: gender, skin color, nationality, language, family economic and educational status, and the like. These social forces, which busily assign position in the societal hierarchy, launch a process of dehumanization. Malcolm X noted how racism socially determined one's future: "When they start indicting us because of our color that means we're indicted before we're born, which is the worst kind of crime that can be committed."[12] In *Pedagogy of the Oppressed*, Paulo Freire calls dehumanization "a *distortion* of the vocation of becoming more fully human [and] the result of an unjust order that engenders violence in the oppressors, which in turn dehumanizes the oppressed."[13]

Malcolm X believed that "the problem of racism was fundamentally one of powerlessness on the part of the oppressed people to affirm and to protect their humanity."[14] He was born into a family that daily experienced racial harassment. Home was not a safe place for Malcolm. The Ku Klux Klan terrorized his family and burned their house to the ground. The psychological ramifications of self-worth and skin color dynamics invaded Malcolm's home life when he experienced his father's favoritism and his mother's disfavor due to his fair complexion. After his father died, the social welfare system offered his mother little support as a poor, widowed, single parent of seven children. Soon, the state removed her from the house, ending any sense of home. Malcolm's psychosocial environment was no better at his school or foster home. At school his teacher could not see a potential lawyer, only a subhuman whose place was in a "menial" job. His foster parents did not see a future leader. Rather, they treated Malcolm as they would a pet. No one recognized Malcolm's intrinsic worth as a human being. He was objectified and stereotyped. Malcolm X lived in a society where the dominant culture defined humanity as white. If you were not white you experienced life as an outsider with little hope for acceptance.

Dehumanization begins when those in power formulate and perpetuate a definition of who is fully human. A hierarchical society defines the dominant group as superior or human and the dominated groups as inferior or subhuman. When power is maintained through a racial hierarchy, "it is the racist who creates his inferior."[15] For Malcolm X, to be fully human in the United States was to be white. Since he could never become white, Malcolm X would never be considered fully human in such a society.

The impact of a racist social system is dehumanization. Malcolm X recounted the effects of racism on his psyche in his autobiography. One revealing scene occurred during his days as a street hustler in Boston, Massachusetts. Malcolm had straightened his hair through a process called a conk, which used lye to burn the hair straight. Malcolm X reflected on the experience: "This was my first really big step toward self-degradation: when I endured all of that pain, literally burning my flesh to have it look like a white man's hair. I had joined that multitude of Negro men and women in America who are brainwashed into believing that the black people are 'inferior'—and white people 'superior'—that they will even violate and mutilate their God-created bodies to try to look 'pretty' by white standards."[16] Malcolm X tried to secure his sense of worth by assimilating as much as was possible to the prevailing definition of value, in this case whiteness. The fact that it was impossible for Malcolm X to be white did not keep him from trying to mimic the image projected as the norm—as "human."

Societal definitions of who is fully human encourage self-degra-dation, but they are not enough to sustain the psychological enslave-ment of an entire people. A systemic process of dehumanization must demean and destroy the culture and history of a people. The destruc-tion of cultural identity damages an entire people. Malcolm X regu-larly taught, "Just as a tree without roots is dead, a people without history or cultural roots also becomes a dead people.... Once our names were taken and our language was taken and our identity was destroyed and our roots were cut off with no history, we became like a stump, something dead."[17]

In addition to defining the essence of humanness as white and denying the worth of persons of color and their cultures, a further step stigmatizes and criminalizes oppressed people. Malcolm X stated, "Victims of racism are created in the image of racists. When the victims struggle vigorously to protect themselves from the vio-lence of others, they are made to appear in the image of criminals; as the criminal image is projected onto the victim."[18] Dehumanization causes persons to internalize the oppression that has been projected onto them by the dominant society. According to Malcolm X:

As these Europeans dominated the continent of Africa, it was they who created the image of Africa that was projected abroad. And they projected Africa and the people of Africa in a negative image, a hateful image. They made us think that Africa was a land of jungle, a land of animals, a land of can-nibals and savages. . . . You can't hate your origin and not end up hating yourself. And since we all originated in Africa, you can't make us hate Africa without making us hate ourselves. . . . We ended up with twenty-two million black people here in America who hated everything about us that was African. . . . We hated our hair. We hated our nose, the shape of our nose, and the shape of our lips, the color of our skin. . . . As long as we hated those people, we hated ourselves. As long as we hated what we thought they looked like, we hated what we actually looked like. . . . When you teach a man to hate his lips, the lips that God gave him, the shape of the nose that God gave him, the texture of the hair that God gave him, the color of the skin that God gave him, you've committed the worst crime that a race of people can commit. . . . Our color became a chain, a psychological chain. Our blood—African blood—became a psychological chain, a prison, because we were ashamed of it. . . . We felt trapped because our skin was Black. We felt trapped because we had African blood in our veins.[19]

In his study on the impact of European colonization, Frantz Fanon described the internalization of racism. "I begin to suffer from not being a white man to the degree that the white man imposes discrimination on me, makes me a colonized native, robs me of all worth, all individuality, tells me I am a parasite on the world, that I must bring myself as quickly as possible into step with the white world." Fanon realized that in the midst of the pressure of dehumanization, the oppressed person exhibits the psychological and spiritual need for some recognition. "Then I will quite simply try to make myself white: that is, I will compel the white man to acknowledge that I am a human."[20] Dehumanization is complete when a person is dependent on the oppressor for her or his identity.

A system that oppresses and demeans a certain group of people will also damage the humanity of the creators and guardians of the system, as well as those who materially benefit from its existence. A contemporary of Fanon, Aimé Césaire observes that colonization "dehumanizes even the most civilized man; that colonial activity, colonial enterprise, colonial conquest, which is based on contempt for the native and justified by that contempt, inevitably tends to change him who undertakes it; that the colonizer, who in order to ease his conscience gets into the habit of seeing the other man as *an animal*, accustoms himself to treating him like an animal, and tends objectively to transform *himself* into an animal."[21]

Césaire points out that the process of oppression also dehumanizes the victimizer. Can the Nazis be considered fully human given the Holocaust of the Jews? Can slave masters in the United States be considered fully human given the brutality of slavery? Can the military dictators in Burma be considered fully human given their orders to kill by the thousands innocent nonviolent protesters? They are humans whose acts of inhumanity diminish their very selves. Oppressing and demeaning others reflects back on the perpetrator—

the one in power—and impoverishes her or his soul. The evil of the social structure ensnares both oppressor and oppressed.

It is not only the creators or rulers of unjust systems who are dehumanized by oppression. All who participate in or benefit from the ruling system are contaminated to some degree. Dietrich Bonhoeffer was infected by the racism that produced Nazi Germany. As Bonhoeffer gained a clearer vision of the racism that beset Germany, his frustration and righteous indignation grew because he saw racism's tentacles everywhere, even in himself. (He quickly recognized this in his refusal to officiate at the funeral for the Jewish father-in-law of his twin sister.) The Christian churches collaborated in the persecution of the Jews. Some Christian traditions had deemphasized Jesus' humanity—stripping him of his Jewishness and blaming Jews for his death—making it easier for Nazism to persuade the majority of the churches in Germany to purge their congregations of any Jewish individuals. Even many of Bonhoeffer's beloved seminarians and fellow pastors of the underground Confessing Church enlisted in the German military to defend this unjust system.

Systemic injustice dehumanizes both the powerful and the powerless. Faith-inspired activists must recognize that they are struggling for liberation within structures that define and shape reality. Therefore, their own lives and leadership are personally affected. Mystic-activists seek to rediscover their own lost sense of humanity in order to move with others toward liberation and healing. They also help dismantle systems that dehumanize societies and rebuild them in community, using the tools of justice and peace.

Restoring the Human Identity of Those Oppressed

Malcolm X's unconscious desire to be like whites—the dominant group—was an internal cry to be respected as a fully human person. Since he was operating from a definition that equated humanness with whiteness, the more he tried to look and act like a white person, the closer he thought he was to being accepted as a human being. Paulo Freire observed this tendency among oppressed people in South America, "Their ideal is to be men; but for them, to be men is to be oppressors. This is their model for humanity."[22] This faulty internalized definition of humanity imposed by a racist or oppressive social system has to be rejected for our true humanity to be reclaimed.

Cornel West calls for a "psychic conversion" in order to address such identity confusion. "Malcolm X's notion of psychic conversion holds that black people must no longer view themselves through white lenses. He claims that black people will never value themselves as long as they subscribe to a standard of valuation that devalues them."[23] Malcolm X first experienced a psychic conversion through the Nation of Islam. He stated in a speech, "The religion that The Honorable Elijah Muhammad is teaching us here in America today, is designed to undo in our minds what the white man has done to us. It's designed to undo the type of brain-washing that we have had to undergo for four hundred years at the hand of the white man."[24] Malcolm X discovered that "Elijah Muhammad's version of Islam contained a deconstructive function."[25] His participation in the Nation of Islam brought freedom "from the stigma of 'niggerness'" and "a liberation from the psychological castration and dehumanization" of racism in the United States.[26] Through Elijah Muhammad and the Nation of Islam, Malcolm X was able to reject the dominant culture's definition of humanity and rediscover his self-worth.

Malcolm X regained a sense of his own value through his conversion in prison, and "with the help of the racist doctrine, strict code, and exclusive society of the Black Muslims, he was able to transcend and reject the oppressive values of the white world that were at the foundation of his own self-hatred."[27] Upon his release from prison, Malcolm X saw this kind of positive self-esteem among members of the temple of the Nation of Islam in Detroit. "I had never dreamed of anything like that atmosphere among black people who learned to be proud they were black, who learned to love other black people instead of being jealous and suspicious."[28]

As a leader, Malcolm X also understood that personal worth needed to be enhanced by cultural esteem. His reading in prison informed him that Africa was not a place of shame. Rather it should be a source of pride for African Americans. Malcolm X's constant rhetoric regarding the splendor of Africa's history and culture "was a means by which African Americans could reclaim their psyches and their self-respect in order to fight back against racism and exploitation in the Western hemisphere."[29]

Malcolm X traveled to several countries in Africa during the last year of his life. His journeys across the continent served as a living compass to reorient African Americans toward a vital cultural and historical link. Through connecting the struggle of African Americans with "the liberation struggle in Africa, Malcolm was creating a pride in Africa, and a sense of African identity."[30]

The recovery of what has been lost in the process of dehumanization is essential for restoring a healthy identity. Even though Malcolm X gained much from his time in the Nation of Islam, it could not complete his restoration to a human identity. As Cornel West contends, the Nation of Islam was primarily a response to white supremacy. In fact it "was predicated on an obsession with white supremacy." West writes:

> This preoccupation with white supremacy still allowed white people to serve as the principal point of reference. That which fundamentally motivates one still dictates the terms of what one thinks and does—so the motivation of a black supremacist doctrine reveals how obsessed one is with white supremacy. This is understandable in a white racist society—but it is crippling for a despised people struggling for freedom, in that one's eyes should be on the prize, not on the perpetuator of one's oppression.[31]

The Nation of Islam did not have the worldview to completely free Malcolm X. His sense of identity was not yet disconnected from whiteness. Malcolm X's exit from the Nation of Islam and its ideology allowed him to think about identity in fresh ways. He exhibited a sign of healthy esteem when, through his Mecca pilgrimage, "human" became his primary identifier.

An identity rooted in humanity includes racial, sexual, cultural, and other sources of distinctiveness. Yet it also transcends these temporal identifiers. Faith-inspired activists who emerge from the margins need to embark on a long journey of healing from the deep psychic and spiritual scars oppression leaves. Those who continue to be bruised by the daily reality of racism and injustice accept that this is a lifetime process. Without restoring her or his sense of an identity rooted in humanity, a liberation leader easily becomes the next oppressor. Far too many dictatorial leaders or oppressive systems result from the deep pain of prior victimization. Mystic-activists need to be constantly aware of this possibility as they seek to move with others toward a healed identity.

Mystic-activists find a passion and energy for others because of the fruits of their own healing. Native American activist Winona LaDuke states: "Coming from where I came from, the government process of trying to deny Native people our own identity is such a horrible process that it means most people are faced with a lot of extra problems. That process of trying to reclaim identity and rebuild community—because in reclaiming identity one has to heal your community, where you're from—has really engaged me in the process of social activism."[32]

Restoring the Human Identity of the Oppressor

Mystic-activists from privileged backgrounds must take a journey toward healing that differs from their less privileged counterparts. Paulo Freire wrote that for some who sat in seats of power, "even when the contradiction is resolved authentically by a new situation established by the liberated laborers, the former oppressors do not feel liberated. On the contrary, they genuinely consider themselves to be oppressed." Freire observed:

> Conditioned by the experience of oppressing others, any situation other than their former seems to them like oppression. Formerly, they could eat, dress, wear shoes, be educated, travel, and hear Beethoven; while millions did not eat, had no clothes or shoes, neither studied nor traveled, much less listened to Beethoven. Any restriction on this way of life, in the name of the rights of the community, appears to the former oppressors as a profound violation of their individual rights.[33]

Privilege gained through injustice appears to be "normal" to those in power. The loss of privilege and power, even when agreed to by members of a dominant group, causes a dramatic change. It is easy to favor social change if it does not require any personal change or sacrifice. But in order to attain equity and justice—to improve the quality of life for those oppressed or poor—the lives of the privileged will be affected.

Those among the dominant culture, or the privileged, who desire liberation need people from the margins to help them find freedom. The humanization process of an oppressor occurs only by engaging with the oppressed. Social justice activists need this to complete their healing. Dietrich Bonhoeffer's identity was redeemed because of his encounters with people who had suffered the effects of racism in Harlem and anti-Semitism in Germany. Bonhoeffer would never have recognized his own blindness to injustice without the help of those for whom oppression was a daily reality. His comfortable life as an academic and pastor shielded him from the realities at the margins. Bonhoeffer chose to build relationships with persons who were oppressed, and those relationships helped him discover an identity rooted in common humanity.

Mystic-activists infected by dominant-culture privileges—even when they have deep, intimate relationships with persons who have experienced oppression in society—need to embrace the fact that healing is a long-term process. When people "cease to be exploiters or indifferent spectators or simply the heirs of exploitation and move to the side of the exploited, they almost always bring with them the marks of their origin: their prejudices and their deformations, which include a lack of confidence in the people's ability to think, to want, and to know." Even with the best of intentions to see society change, "because of their background they believe that they must be the executors of the transformation."[34] Mystic-activists raised in privilege have to learn to trust people who live under oppression and even follow their lead in creating a healthier society.

In order to remain free from the "marks of their origin," mystic-activists from privileged backgrounds need to find solidarity with the people at the margins. It is not enough for mystic-activists from places of privilege to visit the communities of oppressed people occasionally. It is not enough for faith-inspired leaders raised in the dominant culture to invite persons from the margins to join them for conversations in places of comfort. Mystic-activists must have ongoing relationships with many persons from marginalized communities. Mystic-activists raised in privilege need to engage in such relationships for the duration of their lives—so powerful is the lure of privilege and so long is the shadow of power.

Mystic-Activists and the Process of Humanizing Society

Mystic-activists engage in the process of humanization, their own and that of others, from a profoundly spiritual place. Dietrich Bonhoeffer claimed that humanization was at the center of Christian theology. "Christ has taken on this *human form....* In Christ's incarnation all of humanity regains the dignity of bearing the image of God. Whoever from now on attacks the least of the people attacks Christ, who took on human form and who in himself has restored the image of God for all who bear a human countenance."[35] Bonhoeffer was making a "subtle reference to the Jewish victims of Nazi genocide."[36]

Aung San Suu Kyi notes the centrality of humanity in Buddhism, which "places the greatest value on man, who alone of all beings can achieve the supreme state of Buddhahood. Each man has in him the potential to realize the truth through his own will and endeavour and to help others realize it. Human life therefore is infinitely precious."[37]

The military junta in Burma attempts to persuade people that human rights is not a spiritual or moral issue. Suu Kyi reflects, "It was predictable that as soon as the issue of human rights became an integral part of the movement for democracy the official media should start ridiculing and condemning the whole concept of human rights, dubbing it a western artifact alien to traditional values. [This] was also ironic [given that] Buddhism [is] the foundation of traditional Burmese culture."[38]

As people in the midst of being healed at a deep level, mystic-activists can embody a human way of living in an unjust world. They show love and care for those at the margins struggling to withstand the frontal assault to their dignity and personhood. Suu Kyi embodies a love for the Burmese people, a willingness to "risk her own freedom to fight for theirs, [and] a gift for understanding and embracing the pain of others as if it were her own."[39] An elderly man standing in the rain outside the house of Aung San Suu Kyi said, "We come here because we know that we are the most important thing in the world to her. She cares about us."

Mystic-activists also model how to forgive and even help redeem the oppressor because their healthy human identity allows them to recognize that the oppressor is also human. Aung San Suu Kyi demonstrated this when asked how she felt about those who ordered her house arrest. "I liked most of them as human beings—I could never help seeing the human side of them, what is likable. This is not to say I liked what they did. There are lots of things that they did and they are doing which I do not like at all. You must not think that I was very angelic and never got angry. Of course I got angry. But I never lost sight of the fact that they were human beings. And like all human beings, there's a side to them which must be likable."[40] Suu Kyi adds, "To forgive, I think, basically means the ability to see the person apart from the deed and to recognize that although he has done that deed, it does not mean that he is irredeemable."[41]

At the end of his life, Malcolm X's passion for ministry was moving from an exclusive focus on African Americans to a more inclusive focus that encompassed the needs of other persons of color, and even whites. Had Malcolm X lived, his focus might have paralleled that of one who was sitting in a South African prison at that same time. Perhaps Malcolm X would have echoed Nelson Mandela's words, "My hunger for the freedom of my own people became a hunger for the freedom of all people, white and black." Mandela points out, "The oppressed and the oppressor alike are robbed of their humanity." All who follow the call to mystic-activism and journey toward healing meet Mandela's vision on the way: "When I walked out of prison, that was my mission, to liberate the oppressed and the oppressor both."[42]

Aung San Suu Kyi, 1999

© Reuters/Corbis

7

AUNG SAN SUU KYI:
"A REVOLUTION OF THE SPIRIT"

She is known throughout Burma simply as "the Lady." This title of respect and affection bestowed upon Aung San Suu Kyi is not meant to diminish her significance or soften her revolutionary status—as it might seem to those outside of Burma. When Barbara Victor was researching her biography on Suu Kyi, she asked her cab driver if he thought she needed to visit Suu Kyi, given all of the security measures put in place by the government to limit access to her. The cab driver replied, "The Lady is Burma. She encompasses the hopes and dreams of the people. If you don't talk to her, you will never understand the true tragedy of my country."[1]

Aung San Suu Kyi is a faith-inspired leader who has embraced an ethics of revolution that says systemic change in society requires an internally driven change in values. Suu Kyi proclaims, "Without a revolution of the spirit, the forces which produced the iniquities of the old order would continue to be operative, posing a constant threat to the process of reform and regeneration."[2]

The Daughter of a Hero of Modern Burma

Aung San Suu Kyi was born on June 19, 1945, during a time of great political change in Burma. Her father, Aung San, was at the center of historic events in the country. For much of the nineteenth century and the first four decades of the twentieth century Burma was considered part of India under the colonial rule of Great Britain. A new constitution created a separate British Burma in 1937. Four years later, Burmese freedom fighters allied with Japanese military forces to overthrow British colonial rule—shortly after Japan had attacked Pearl Harbor. General Aung San led the Burmese Independence Army in the struggle for liberation. The Japanese allowed Burma to create the Burma National Army under the leadership of General Aung San and General Ne Win. What they believed would be independence turned out to be Japanese occupation. The Chinese Nationalists and the Allied military forces of Great Britain and the United States attacked the Japanese armies in Burma during the final days of World War II in 1945. Aung San led the Burma National Army in what appeared to be an attack against the Allies. As the Burmese military arrived in Allied-held regions, however, they joined the Allies to free Burma from Japanese occupation.

When World War II ended, Aung San staunchly refused to allow Burma to return permanently to British colonial rule. Over the next few years, he negotiated with Great Britain for independence on behalf of Burma. On January 27, 1947, Aung San signed an agreement with British prime minister Clement Attlee stating that Burma would move toward democratic elections and independence in less than a year. Aung San declared his vision for an independent Burma: "A nation is a conglomeration of races and religions that should develop a nationalism that is common with the welfare of one and all, irrespective of race, religion, class, or sex."[3]

The Burmese elected a constitutional assembly in June 1947. Just over a month later, Aung San and six other leaders were assassinated while in a cabinet meeting. The killings were orchestrated by U Saw, the last puppet prime minister under British colonial rule. Aung San had widely been regarded as the person who would be Burma's first democratically elected prime minister. He was dead at thirty-two years of age. Aung San's vision of an independent Burma was not derailed. Independence came on January 4, 1948. One of Aung San's colleagues who survived the assassinations, U Nu, became the first—and so far only—democratically elected prime minister of Burma.

Democracy did not come easy for Burma. There was much turmoil in the country in the years that followed. Then in 1962,

General Ne Win, who had been Aung San's partner in the formation of the Burma National Army, led a military coup. Ne Win and his followers dismantled democracy and declared Ne Win the "supreme legislative, executive, and judicial authority."[4] The vision for Burma promoted by Aung San was never realized in the twentieth century.

In the late 1980s, Aung San's daughter, Aung San Suu Kyi, would once again raise the banner of her father's vision—a father she had last seen when she was but two years old. This time, Aung San Suu Kyi would call for a revolution of the spirit.

Years of Preparation

Khin Kyi, Aung San's wife, joined the government in her husband's place, serving in various roles while also raising three small children. Tragedy visited this family again in 1953, when one of her sons drowned at the age of nine. In 1960, two years before the coup, Khin Kyi was appointed as Burma's ambassador to India. Aung San Suu Kyi was seventeen years old and in school in India when the coup occurred. She studied and embraced the nonviolent philosophy of Mahatma Gandhi while in India. Suu Kyi left India for England in 1964, at age nineteen, to study at Oxford University. At Oxford, Suu Kyi expanded her knowledge of nonviolence to include Martin Luther King Jr. and the Civil Rights Movement of the United States.

Suu Kyi pursued an academic life of teaching and research after graduating from Oxford University. The primary focus of Aung San Suu Kyi's scholarship was her country of origin, Burma. She moved to New York City and began a job at the United Nations two years later, in 1969. During the 1970s and 1980s, Suu Kyi continued her studies and research in the United States, England, Bhutan, Japan, and India. On January 1, 1972, she married a fellow academic, Englishman Michael Aris, in a Buddhist ceremony in England. They had two sons, born in 1973 and 1977.

Buddhist monk Rewata Dhamma, visited Suu Kyi in 1977 and "had the distinct impression that Daw Suu Kyi was preparing herself in the event her country needed her."[5] ("Daw" is a title of respect for women. "U" is a title for men.) That same year, Suu Kyi turned thirty-two years old. This was the age that her father was when he was killed, and "those close to Suu claim that there was almost a mystical awareness of her loss."[6] In 1984, she published a biography of her father.

Return to Burma

The year 1988 would transform the life of Aung San Suu Kyi and propel her into the midst of the struggle for reform in her homeland—as though she had always been planning for this time. Suu Kyi's mother had retired to Burma in 1967. By 1988, Suu Kyi and her family had settled into a serene life in England. Her husband, Michael Aris, was a professor at Oxford University. Suu Kyi was enrolled in postgraduate studies.

Aris described what happened on March 31: "Our sons were already in bed and we were reading when the telephone rang. Suu picked up the phone to learn that her mother had suffered a severe stroke. She put the phone down and at once began to pack. I had a premonition that our lives would change forever. Two days later Suu was many thousands of miles away at her mother's bedside in Rangoon."[7]

A few weeks prior to Suu Kyi's arrival, the still reigning military dictatorship of General Ne Win had violently quelled student unrest. On March 12, 1988, an argument had occurred between a number of students from the Rangoon Institute of Technology and the son of the owner of a teahouse located near the institute. In the heat of the argument, the owner's son stabbed a student named Win Myint. The police released the owner's son the next day. The students protested, calling for justice. Riot police arrived to disperse the crowd. The student protest turned into a raucous mob throwing rocks and bottles at the police. In the attempt to subdue the mob, the police shot a student.

The death of this student released the pent up rage from years of dictatorship and oppression. What began as an argument in a teahouse turned into a mass protest against the government. Students called for economic reform and the end of government sponsored violence and oppressive policies. Other university students and concerned citizens joined the Rangoon Institute of Technology students for several days of protests. It is estimated that twelve thousand to fifteen thousand people participated in the protests, with the police and army killing over two hundred. They also arrested, beat, and raped many others.

By the time that Aung San Suu Kyi arrived to care for her mother, the unrest had quieted. Suu Kyi focused all her time and energy on her mother's declining condition. On May 9, the government announced that only three students had died in the crackdown on the protests. This cover-up prompted students from several universities to return to the streets in demonstrations. Through June and July, the protesters increased in number. Many others joined the university students, including high school students. In an unprecedented move, Buddhist monks participated in the protests. Political involvement by monks had not been allowed for hundreds of years.

General Ne Win shocked the nation on July 23, 1988, when in a televised speech he announced that he was retiring after twenty-six years of leading the country and his party. He said, "The world is changing and what we have done has made the country suffer. As chairman of the party I am responsible, and so I offer my resignation. I am leaving the party and leaving politics."[8] In his speech, he called for a referendum on whether the future of the government should be a one-party or multiparty system.

The populace of Burma welcomed Ne Win's announcement. It seemed that freedom might become a reality in the near future. Ne Win's party did not support his remarks. They refused his call for a referendum on Burma's future and quickly named as president Sein Lwin, one of Ne Win's followers. This was an inflammatory selection. Sein Lwin was blamed for the killings of demonstrators in March. The new president moved swiftly to counter Ne Win's referendum talk. Aung San Suu Kyi reflected later, "The frustrations that the people of Burma had been holding back for some two decades erupted and they poured out on to the streets in a great, spontaneous demonstration of their desire for a governing system that would respect their will. The movement for democracy had begun."[9] Millions of people marched peacefully throughout the country in protest of the new administration's maintenance of authoritarian rule. These protests became a daily occurrence by the first week of August 1988. The people proclaimed the name of Aung San, the father of Suu Kyi, as a symbol of the freedom desired by the people and often displayed his photo.

August 8, 1988

On the first day of August, the All Burma Students' Democratic League issued a call for a national strike by all citizens of Burma one week later. The date for the strike was August 8, 1988, or 8-8-88, considered a lucky number. Sein Lwin's government declared martial law and banned all public assemblies. The demonstrators continued to hold rallies as the eighth day of the eighth month approached. Nearly fifty percent of the adults living in the capital city of Rangoon (Yangon) participated. The military arrested many of the protestors.

When the morning of the nationwide strike arrived, "at 8 minutes past 8 in the morning of August 8, 1988, Rangoon dockworkers struck, walking off their jobs *en masse*."[10] Students, lawyers, Buddhist monks, children, civil servants, doctors, and many other concerned citizens joined them in mass demonstrations across the country. This massive outpouring reflected the desire for freedom and witnessed to the people's hope for a better future. Aung San Suu Kyi summed up the day:

> Participating in these peaceful demonstrations were people of all ages, from all different strata of society; students, farmers, labourers, civil servants, including numbers of the armed forces, Buddhist monks, Christians, Muslims, intellectuals, professionals, businessmen, small traders, housewives and artists. Their united demand was for change: they wanted no more of the authoritarian rule, initiated by a military coup in 1962, that had impoverished Burma intellectually, politically, morally and economically.[11]

Marches and rallies occurred throughout the entire day. As evening came, the military moved in and began shooting into the crowd. Suu Kyi reflected on this turn of events, "It is never easy to convince those who have acquired power forcibly of the wisdom of peaceful change."[12] The military killed thousands that night and more over the next four days as demonstrations continued. The soldiers had no regard for the peaceful protestors. They shot students, children, Buddhist monks, and many others. According to estimates, starting on 8-8-88, over three thousand people died in Burma in what was called the Four Eights Massacres. Most people around the world were unaware of the massacres in Burma "because the soldiers had standing orders to shoot on sight anyone with a camera."[13] Less than a year later, similar horrible events in Tiananmen Square in China would gain much broader press attention.

In the midst of massive protests and violent repression, the new president, Sein Lwin, resigned under pressure from the military in an attempt to calm the unrest. Dr. Maung Maung, a civilian and a loyal supporter of Ne Win, replaced him. Maung was the first nonmilitary president since before Ne Win seized power in 1962. Dr. Maung ended martial law and informed the public that Ne Win's request for a referendum on the future of Burma would be honored. Hope for democracy remained strong.

Aung San Suu Kyi Joins the Struggle

Aung San Suu Kyi followed the events in her country from the bedside of her ailing mother. Her presence in Burma was becoming known and "many people believed that the presence of General Aung San's daughter in Burma meant that more than fifty years of repression, civil unrest, and violence would end."[14] Suu Kyi was troubled by the violent repression of the people's heartfelt desire for freedom and democracy. In the violence-filled days following the strike on August 8, Aung San Suu Kyi and a colleague penned a letter to the government of Burma. This open letter was released to the public on August 18 and called for the formation of an independent committee to guide the country toward multiparty elections. The letter responded to General Ne Win's words from his retirement speech of July 23 when he proclaimed, "I believe the 1988 March and June bloodshed and disturbances were meant...to show lack of confidence in Government and the Party behind the Government.... Holding a national referendum on what [the people] wish—a one-party system or a multi-party system—would bring out the answer."[15] The letter quoted Ne Win's words, "If we should have to choose between the good of the party and the good of the nation we should choose the good of the nation."[16]

On August 24, Aung San Suu Kyi made her first public appearance since arriving in Burma in early April. She only spoke a few words at a rally at Rangoon General Hospital announcing that she would give a speech at the Shwedagon Pagoda two days later, on the twenty-sixth of August. The Shwedagon Pagoda is the most sacred Buddhist site in Burma, believed to date back to the time of the Buddha himself. Symbolically, there was no more powerful location for a speech from a woman who would encourage Burma to embrace a revolution of the spirit.

The next day, people began arriving at the pagoda and camping out on the lawn to ensure a spot near the speaker. By the time Aung San Suu Kyi arrived on August 26, between five hundred thousand and a million people had gathered. In her speech, she linked the present struggle to that of her father's day (as many others present had done by carrying his picture and speaking his name). She declared, "I could not, as my father's daughter, remain indifferent to all that was going on. This national crisis could in fact be called the second struggle for national independence."[17] Some who were there remembered the time in 1947 when her father stood on those same steps of the Shwedagon Pagoda and called for liberation from Great Britain. Several foreign journalists spoke "of the 'mystical awe' in which Aung San Suu Kyi, as Aung San's daughter, [was] regarded by the common people."[18] In her speech at the Shwedagon Pagoda, Suu Kyi proclaimed values that were easily recognized as those of her father: "personal commitment, discipline, unity, non-violence and the restoration of basic human rights—and especially multi-party democracy."[19] Suu Kyi moved beyond her father's viewpoint when she added the nonviolent teachings of Gandhi to the message of freedom and democracy in Burma.[20]

The protests continued, often with altercations between protesters and military. In most cases, the demonstrators stayed nonviolent. On one occasion, there was a confrontation in the streets between the military and the peaceful protesters. The army prepared to fire on the crowd of people if they would not end their protest. A boy stepped out from the crowd toward the soldiers. This solitary youthful figure "ripped open his shirt" and presented "his bare chest as a target for the soldiers' weapons." Observers knew from past brutalities that this was a courageous, if not crazy, act of defiance. For some reason on this day "the sight of such a young boy offering his life was too much even for soldiers used to killing."[21] The people prevailed, and the protest went on.

Burma began to descend into anarchy as the protests continued into September 1988. In mid-September, the military ousted the civilian president Dr. Maung Maung before he could hold the promised referendum. The army ruled the country through General Saw Maung. The military established the State Law and Order Restoration Council (SLORC) as the ruling entity in Burma and changed the name of the country in English from the Union of Burma to the Union of Myanmar. The reason given was that Burma is a name from the colonial era. The military cracked down on the protesters, again killing thousands of people, and declared martial law for a second time. General Saw Maung recognized that the demonstrations could not easily be stopped. So he announced that democratic multiparty elections would be held in May 1990. At the same time, the SLORC also banned all public gatherings.

The Election Process

The banning of public events did not discourage or impede Aung San Suu Kyi and her colleagues. The hope implied by the coming elections caused them to immediately form the National League for Democracy (NLD)— one of more than two hundred new political parties that registered for the highly anticipated May 1990 election.

The ruling military government, the SLORC, established the National Unity Party.

Suu Kyi described the process of creating a political party and promoting a multiparty system in a country with little tradition of democracy: "We listened to the voice of the people, that our policies might be in harmony with their legitimate needs and aspirations. We discussed with them the problems of our country and explained why, in spite of its inevitable flaws, we considered democracy to be better than other political systems. Most important of all, we sought to make them understand why we believed that political change was best achieved through non-violent means."[22]

Aung San Suu Kyi became a unifying force for the more than two hundred opposition parties. Although she had little political experience, she had the vision of her father and a commitment to human rights and democracy. She also had the love and respect of the people. Suu Kyi campaigned for freedom and democracy. Sometimes she would speak in more than ten villages in a day. Family friend and diplomat Ma Than E described Suu Kyi's ability to communicate her message: "She has a perfect command of the English language more than matched by her brilliant and inspired use of Burmese. With Burmese she reaches the hearts and minds of her people, like her father before her. With English she interprets her ideas and actions to the world. The first is of more immediate importance in her effort to awake a people sunk in the apathy of years and only recently roused to protest."[23]

In late December 1988, Aung San Suu Kyi's mother died, at the age of seventy-five. Khin Kyi's funeral was held on January 2, 1989, and "a spirit of unity prevailed throughout Rangoon for the first time in decades." The SLORC publicly announced that all citizens of Burma could "freely and without restriction" attend the "funeral of the widow of Burma's national hero."[24] The leader of the military government, General Saw Maung, also attended the event. The nearly one hundred thousand people waited peacefully along the streets of Rangoon to catch a glimpse of the funeral procession. After the funeral, the SLORC returned to its harassment and arrests of persons promoting democracy.

No longer busy with her mother's care, Suu Kyi became even more engaged in the campaign for democracy. The SLORC tried many tactics to discourage her efforts. Armed troops were often present when she spoke. Military vehicles would drive ahead of her campaign organization and tell people not to attend her speeches. They would play loud music so people could not hear Suu Kyi's speeches. Fences were erected to keep citizens from attending her rallies. The government prohibited the NLD's campaign signs. It was insinuated that she had communist ties. The army passed out cartoons "alleging that she indulged in abnormal sexual practices and had several husbands."[25]

In April 1989, as Aung San Suu Kyi and some of her followers were walking on a road during a campaign visit, they were ordered by a military officer to stop. When they kept walking, "six soldiers under the command of an Army captain jumped down from a jeep, assumed a kneeling position, and took aim at her." Suu Kyi directed the people with her to step aside to the sidewalk, and she continued walking down the center of the street as the military men aimed their guns at her. Aung San Suu Kyi commented at the time, "It seemed so much simpler to provide them with a single target than to bring everyone else in. It was at this point that a major ordered the captain to revoke the shooting orders."[26] In an interview much later, Suu Kyi reflected, "Now as for my walking toward the guns . . . I sometimes think that the whole thing has been exaggerated a bit. They were sitting there pointing their guns, and one didn't really have much choice. You either kept walking or you retreated. And if you're not prepared to retreat, you just keep walking. That's all."[27]

Throughout June and July 1989, tens of thousands of people gathered at each rally where Aung San Suu Kyi spoke. She presented Mahatma Gandhi and Martin Luther King Jr. as models of how they should proceed in their direct action campaign for democratic change in Burma. The momentum was on her side. Yet the opposition parties grew concerned that the military government might not follow through on their promise of elections. On July 3, Suu Kyi called for talks between the SLORC and the political parties to discuss the elections. She consistently held out hope for peaceful and constructive dialogue regarding the future of Burma. The SLORC refused her invitation. In an interview that took place on July 8, she expressed her belief that the former dictator, General Ne Win, was still leading the government from behind the scenes and had no interest in dialogue. Suu Kyi appealed to the military informing them "that they have been made to play the role of thugs, to make sure that a few old men can remain in power."[28]

Aung San Suu Kyi often delivered her message of freedom by holding rallies on days of symbolic importance. A major event was planned for Martyrs' Day, the anniversary of the assassinations of her father and the cabinet, celebrated annually on the nineteenth of July. Suu Kyi planned to declare publicly her belief that Ne Win still controlled the military and had no intentions of ceding power to a civilian government. She announced her plans to lead a mass demonstration on the forty-second anniversary of her father's death. The government responded by mobilizing the military and moving into the streets to prevent the protests. The government recognized that Aung San Suu Kyi was a threat to their power. Suu Kyi cancelled the demonstration knowing that a confrontation with the army would lead to bloodshed. Commenting on the decision later, she said, "Well, it was not an easy decision to make. I realized that I would not get hurt...others would have. To carry on would have been irresponsible. If others would have got hurt and I had remained unhurt, it would have been a responsibility I could not have lived with."[29] Suu Kyi spent the anniversary of her father's death at home.

The day following Martyrs' Day, July 20, 1989, the government placed Aung San Suu Kyi under house arrest. She had tried to leave the house to lay flowers at her father's grave but was not allowed. During the morning, eleven trucks full of soldiers arrived at Suu Kyi's home and blocked off the street. In the afternoon, they entered and began to search her house. The phone lines were cut. Several other members of the NLD were arrested and taken to prison. Suu Kyi was held as a prisoner in her own home. Her two teenage sons were with her that day, while her husband was in Scotland for his father's funeral. He traveled to Burma as soon as possible. She immediately began a hunger strike in order to call attention to the plight of those arrested. The hunger strike lasted for two weeks, until the government assured her that they would treat those arrested fairly. In early September, Suu Kyi's husband and their two sons returned to England. It would be a few years before they would see each other again.

The election process continued without the public presence of Aung San Suu Kyi and most of the leadership of the NLD. While under house arrest, in December 1989, Suu Kyi allowed her name to be entered as a candidate for a seat in a new government. The military's political party challenged her candidacy in February 1990, claiming that she was a dissident. Her name did not appear on the final ballot.

Elections were held in May 1990. This was probably the only promise that the military regime did not renege on. To the shock of the nation, Aung San Suu Kyi's party, the National League for Democracy won 392 of the 485 legislative seats available—more than 80 percent. When combined with other opposition parties, the vote against the military sponsored party came to 98 percent of the seats. According to public opinion in Burma and throughout the world, this was a victory for freedom and democracy—and a victory for the leadership of Aung San Suu Kyi.

The SLORC refused to recognize the election of a civilian government. In the days that followed the elections, the SLORC informed the populace that the election had not been for a new government. Rather, the purpose of the election was to elect persons who would represent the people at a National Convention to develop a new constitution. (At this writing, there is still not a new constitution in Burma.) The SLORC also took additional measures to ensure that Aung San Suu Kyi could never be elected to the country's leadership. The SLORC pointed to a clause in the constitution that did not allow for a person to become president who was married to a foreigner or had been out of Burma longer than twenty years. The NLD responded that these clauses were added by the SLORC just before the 1990 elections. They were not in the original documents. Suu Kyi responded, "It always seemed ridiculous that the government would rewrite a clause in the constitution to apply just to one specific individual."[30] This action clearly demonstrated the threat that Aung San Suu Kyi was to the ruling military junta.

The Leader of a Revolution of the Spirit

One can ponder how Aung San Suu Kyi emerged as the leader of this revolutionary movement for freedom in Burma. In the introduction to Aung San Suu Kyi's book, *Freedom from Fear*, Michael Aris wrote of the leadership that his wife Suu Kyi offered Burma: "She brought overwhelming unity to a spontaneous, hitherto leaderless revolt. She insisted at all times that the movement should be based on a non-violent struggle for human rights as the primary object. She spoke to the common people of her country as they had not been spoken to for so long—as individuals worthy of love and respect."[31]

Historian Phillip Kreager suggests that Aung San Suu Kyi's leadership in this revolution of the spirit was the result of three factors: (1) the historical fact that she was the daughter of Aung San—"the unquestioned architect of independent Burma in the modern period"; (2) the strong identification with the legacy of her father and the haunting possibility that she might experience a similar fate (Suu Kyi's years of house arrest have enhanced the iconic power of her symbolic stature as the leader of the movement—like Mandela's long imprisonment in South Africa); and (3) the hope she provides Burma through "the guidance she has brought to a highly unstable situation, sustained by the personal force, courage and sound judgment manifest in her words and actions...."[32]

Aung San Suu Kyi's guidance was consistent. She insisted on the "restoration of human rights—freedom of speech, of assembly, of political organization, of information, free elections, freedom from fear." Human rights were the prelude to any possible reform. She was the first person who "introduced the issue of human rights into Burmese political discussion." Suu Kyi promoted nonviolence as the only process that could lead to the just and humane end sought. She believed that a new government must be based on principles rather than on leadership (charismatic or military dictatorship), party divisions, or strategies of coercion. She accepted the army as a security force but rejected its co-optation as a tool for a dictatorial regime. She called for "personal and collective discipline" in the struggle for social change.[33]

House Arrest

Aung San Suu Kyi remained under her first house arrest for six years, before being released in July 1995. During these six years, her husband was a single parent to their two sons and often served as Suu Kyi's voice in the international arena. He edited her book *Freedom from Fear*, published in 1991. Suu Kyi's house arrest was at times very harsh. She initially had no source of income and sold household items just to eat. At one point, she dropped from 106 to 90 pounds due to hunger and illness. Suu Kyi survived the difficulties of house arrest through "a rigorous schedule that included exercise, meditation, reading, playing the piano before it was irreparably out of tune, and listening to the radio.... Up at four every morning, she would tidy up before sitting at the foot of her bed in a half lotus position to meditate for one hour."[34]

Aung San Suu Kyi was free to leave Burma at any time. The government said that Suu Kyi "always had the choice of safe passage out of Burma in a chauffeur-driven car to the airport and a free one-way ticket back to England."[35] She never accepted the offer, knowing that if she left she might never be allowed back into the country. Her commitment to freedom and a future of human rights in Burma meant sacrifice of her own personal freedom. By choosing to remain in Burma, she also gave up any possibility of regular contact with her husband and two sons. She said, "I don't think I will have a normal family life for a very long time."[36] She still has not been reunited with her family.

During her house arrest, the world began to recognize the importance of Aung San Suu Kyi in the struggle for human rights in Burma. In 1991, she was awarded the Nobel Peace Prize. She dared not leave the country, so her sons accepted the award on her behalf. The Nobel Peace Prize brought much greater international awareness of the lack of freedom and the frequent human rights abuses in Burma. Several countries pressured the ruling military regime to recognize the elections of 1990.

The government responded to the increased international attention with more internal repression and persecution of Suu Kyi. Her opponents began to spread rumors throughout Burmese society.

One piece of slander implied that the flowers in her hair symbolized her need for adulation from the masses. It was rumored that her husband used the Nobel Prize money to buy a new house in England. The SLORC regularly reminded the citizens of Burma that Suu Kyi had not lived in Burma as an adult until she came to care for her mother. Therefore, she could not possibly comprehend what the country needed.

A few years after receiving the Nobel Peace Prize, it appeared that the government had changed its position on Aung San Suu Kyi. Two of the SLORC's highest leaders invited her to meet with them at a government residence. This was the first time that she had been able to venture outside of her yard. Government-sponsored television showed the meeting of Suu Kyi and the two generals. As the pictures of Suu Kyi and the smiling generals appeared on the screen, a voice described to the audience watching only what the government wanted them to believe was happening. The appearance of Aung San Suu Kyi with leaders of the SLORC caused Burmese citizens and international leaders to believe that this might be the eve of freedom and reconciliation.

The television broadcast was a public relations event orchestrated to portray the government in a better light. The government had no intention of releasing Aung San Suu Kyi from house arrest. When asked later why she was not released following the meeting, one of the generals said, "We were well aware of the dangers to this country caused by a communist conspiracy. Unfortunately, Aung San Suu Kyi had been thrust into the leadership role unknowingly by people who did not want democracy for Myanmar, but only for themselves.... We love and respect General Aung San and since Suu Kyi is his daughter, we also have a special attachment to her as the daughter of our national hero."[37]

Throughout her years of house arrest, Aung San Suu Kyi remained open to the possibility of dialogue and reconciliation with the SLORC. Buddhist monk Rewata Dhamma was given permission to meet with Suu Kyi a few times. "On my first visit to Suu Kyi, sometime in the summer of 1994 she told me that she wanted national reconciliation. Her exact words were, 'democracy is not something you get from others. You have to build it yourself. If Nelson Mandela could work with whites, I can work with the SLORC.'"[38]

Released from House Arrest

The government released Aung San Suu Kyi from house arrest on July 11, 1995. As word of her new circumstances spread, people gathered in front of her home. Suu Kyi made the following statement:

> I have always believed that the future stability and happiness of our nation depends entirely on the readiness of all parties to work for reconciliation. During the years that I spent under house arrest many parts of the world have undergone almost unbelievable change, and all changes for the better were brought about through dialogue.... Once bitter enemies in South Africa are now working together for the betterment of their people. Why can't we look forward to a similar process? We have to choose between dialogue or utter devastation.[39]

A few days later, she spoke to an even larger crowd and said, "People say there's something new in the fact that I'm calling for a dialogue with the SLORC, but that isn't true. I've always asked for a dialogue. Only discipline and courage devoid of any grudge will help us achieve our desired aims and aspirations. Pro-democracy forces should work slowly, steadily, thoughtfully, and courageously."[40]

The SLORC military junta did not publicly acknowledge her request for dialogue or even note that she had been released. Even though she had some freedom of movement in the country, the government still closely watched her and placed many restrictions on her freedom.

Michael Aris had not been able to visit his wife in two years, because the government of Burma would not grant him a visa. He increased his efforts to travel to Burma when he discovered at age fifty-two that he had cancer. The military dictatorship offered Suu Kyi a visa to go to England but refused Aris's request to come to

Burma. Suu Kyi's husband died on his fifty-third birthday in March 1999. The two had not seen each other for three years.

In September 2000, the government placed Aung San Suu Kyi under house arrest once more. There she remained for nineteen months. At this writing, Suu Kyi is under house arrest yet again. She remains strong in her commitment to freedom and reconciliation. Many years after the unrecognized elections in Burma, Aung San Suu Kyi continues to call for a revolution of the spirit.

8
THE ETHICS OF REVOLUTION

Throughout the Burmese struggle for freedom, Aung San Suu Kyi envisioned a revolution of the spirit. As a faith-inspired activist, she saw that her country needed more than political change. Her vision remained consistent whether she was speaking to crowds of hundreds of thousands or was alone and confined under house arrest. "I have always said that true revolution has to be that of the spirit. You have to be convinced that you need to change certain things—not just material things. You want a political system which is guided by certain spiritual values—values that are different from those that you've lived by before."[1]

Other mystic-activists also share the idea of a revolution of the spirit. Malcolm X reflected on this notion in his autobiography: "Mankind's history has proved from one era to another that the true criterion of leadership is spiritual. Men are attracted by spirit. By power, men are *forced*. Love is engendered by *spirit*. By power, anxieties are created.... The only true world solution today is governments guided by true religion—of the spirit."[2]

Martin Luther King Jr. called for a revolution of values. In a speech, he proclaimed, "I am convinced that if we are to get on the right side of the world revolution, we as a nation must undergo a radical revolution of values." King rejected a materialistic notion of revolution. He continued, "We must rapidly begin the shift from a 'thing-oriented' society to a 'person-oriented' society. When machines and computers, profit motives and property rights, are considered more important than people, the giant triplets of racism, extreme materialism, and militarism are incapable of being conquered."[3]

Before Aung San Suu Kyi, Malcolm X, and King, Mohandas Gandhi had pursued a strategy based on the assumption that "lasting political change is through the inner transformation of masses of individuals."[4] When Aung San Suu Kyi and others call for a revolution of the spirit, they truly believe that "religion can become the spiritual force for revolutionary change."[5]

Those who call for a revolution of the spirit know that the end will reflect the means. For justice and freedom to be the final outcome, justice and freedom must imbue the process all along the way. The ethics and methods of the spiritual revolution itself must match the integrity of the end sought. Malcolm X's cry for freedom and justice "by any means necessary" expressed the urgency felt by those oppressed. But the call for a revolution of the spirit articulates the deeply felt desire for an egalitarian community where the very terms *oppressor* and *oppressed* become unnecessary.

The Most Revolutionary Person on Earth

Dietrich Bonhoeffer proclaimed in a sermon: "The man who loves because he is made free by the truth of God is the most revolutionary person on earth. He is the upsetting of all values, the dynamite of the human society. He is the most dangerous man."[6] Mystic-activists can be called revolutionaries—freed by the truth of their religious faith. Bonhoeffer clearly fit his own definition of a revolutionary person. He embraced his freedom by upsetting the values of the Nazi regime. No one would argue with the contention that Malcolm X was the "dynamite of the human society." He was a revolutionary "both in the sense of a return to a former principle and in the sense of an upheaval."[7] Aung San Suu Kyi is revolutionary in her call for a revolution of the spirit and in her amazing ability to always reach out with love to those who persecute her. As faith-inspired revolutionaries, they join a much too small group. The reality is that "religious institutions have more often played a role supporting established elites than one of rebellion against them, and a revolutionary role is least common of all."[8]

Mystic-activists call for revolution as a response to existing injustice. Malcolm X used a colorful metaphor in a speech to illustrate the need for a revolution for racial justice in the United States:

> It's impossible for a chicken to produce a duck egg even though they both belong to the same family of fowl—a chicken just doesn't have it within its system to produce a duck egg. It can't do it. It can only produce according to what the particular system was constructed to produce. The system in this country cannot produce freedom for an Afro-American. It is impossible for this system, this economic system, this political system, this social system, this system, period. It's impossible for this system as it stands to produce freedom right now for the Black man in this country. And if ever a chicken did produce a duck egg, I'm certain you would say it was certainly a revolutionary chicken![9]

If the system in place cannot produce freedom for all members of the society, then a change is called for.

The purpose of a revolution is "to abolish the present status quo and to attempt to replace it with a qualitatively different one." The aim of a revolution is "a just society based on new relationships of production [and] an end to the domination of some countries by others, of some social classes by others, of some people by others."[10] Martin Luther King Jr. said, "For years I labored with the idea of reforming the existing institutions of the society, a little change here, a little change there. Now I feel quite differently. I think you've got to have a reconstruction of the entire society, a revolution of values."[11] Revolution is about dismantling structures in a society to create a new and more just system. A call for a revolution of the spirit is a call for both societal transformation and individual conversion.

The three principle mystic-activists in this book clearly called for a revolution of the political structures. Malcolm X stated his sentiments in his chicken and duck speech. Dietrich Bonhoeffer was willing to participate in a plot to kill Hitler in order to produce a change in the system. Aung San Suu Kyi regularly calls for democracy rather than military dictatorship. At the same time, they invited their fellow revolutionaries, as well as those opposed to their efforts, to engage in an ongoing revolution of their hearts and minds.[12]

What was said of Malcolm X can be said of other mystic-activists: "He was a revolutionary without an army, or an ideology, or any clear sense of how the revolution was to be waged and what it would do if it won. Malcolm, instead, was a revolutionary of the spirit, which is the most subversive sort of all; he was interested less in overthrowing institutions than in undermining the assumptions on which our institutions have run."[13]

A Faith-Inspired Ethics

How does a mystic-activist determine an ethical code of behavior? Dietrich Bonhoeffer declared from prison: "Whoever wishes to take up the problem of a Christian ethic must be confronted at once with a demand which is quite without parallel. He must from the outset discard as irrelevant the two questions which alone impel him to concern himself with the problem of ethics, 'How can I be good?' and 'How can I do good?' and instead of these he must ask the utterly and totally different question, 'What is the will of God?'"[14]

Bonhoeffer's notion that God's will informs the mystic-activist's revolutionary vision and action is a troublesome notion. Many throughout history claim divine approval for their revolutions and behavior. Adolf Hitler and Osama bin Laden persuaded their followers with the rhetoric of God's will. While Bonhoeffer's suggestion for ethics is disturbing at first glance, it is important to understand that his understanding of God's will is based on his reading of the Bible as God's mandate for social justice and reconciliation. Any claim contrary to the Scriptural call for social justice and reconciliation is not God's will. When mystic-activists speak of ethical behavior as being the same as following God's will, they operate from a prior understanding that God always wills justice and liberation.

Jewish philosopher Emmanuel Levinas echoes Bonhoeffer's sentiments. "To know God means to know what has to be done.... Ethics is not the corollary of the vision of God, it is that very vision."[15] In other words, "God's will" is less of a detailed plan and more of an overall direction for mystic-activists. Malcolm X was "as concerned with redemption as with revolution."[16] The motto of Martin Luther King Jr.'s organization—the Southern Christian Leadership Conference—was "to redeem the soul of America." King and the staff of the SCLC pursued their mission with the assumption that revolution included a spiritual dimension, or as King called it, a revolution of values.

One approach to ethics that lends itself to mystic-activists is called liberation ethics—emerging from liberation theology. Unlike traditional understandings of ethics, liberation ethics "does not aspire to be objective in the abstract sense because it, by definition, arises from within the context of oppression. Liberation ethics then is an advocacy ethic. It claims partiality and preference for the experience of the poor."[17] Liberation theology declares that God is on the side of the poor and oppressed of the world. Therefore, "God's will" for the mystic-activist means to advocate for liberation. The beginning phase of liberation ethics is "a structural analysis of the conditions of poverty and oppression, a description of why the poor are poor." Next, the oppressed themselves are "made aware of their situation." Liberation ethics then requires that those who are oppressed "become the primary agents of personal and social transformation."[18] Liberation ethics is a natural outgrowth of a worldview shaped by an activist's experience at the margins of society.

Christian ethicist Cheryl J. Sanders poses the next question, "What sources of ethical guidance are available for those individuals and groups who have made the transition from victimization to moral agency, that is, for those who are already experiencing liberation?"[19] Her answer is "empowerment ethics." Empowerment ethics engages in "the constructive ethical task of delineating steps to be taken by the oppressed to ensure that the experience of empowerment does not result in assimilation of the most dehumanizing values and behaviors of the oppressing group, and in reduplication of intragroup oppression."[20]

Empowerment ethics calls for "remoralization," whereby "persons who have been demoralized as a consequence of oppression, victimization, and self-destructive acts acquire moral agency and become positioned to make positive contributions to the moral progress of the entire community."[21] For Malcolm X, the central focus of the Nation of Islam was transforming victims of racism and poverty into healthy people. When Malcolm X left the Nation of Islam, he organized Muslim Mosque, Inc. as a faith-based vehicle for moral rehabilitation. Dietrich Bonhoeffer attempted to inoculate his countercultural seminarians against the virus of Nazi seduction as he empowered them to be agents of transformation.

Dietrich Bonhoeffer and Malcolm X did not live to see revolution move to liberation. Aung San Suu Kyi is still calling for revolution. Liberation ethics represents the core of how the three understand the will of God. The call for a revolution of the spirit plants the seeds of empowerment ethics. A revolution of the spirit implies that a liberated people will live by an ethics that is consistent with the freedom they have gained.

Prophetic Leadership

A prophet is a revolutionary. A revolutionary whose understanding of ethics is informed by a sense of God's will for liberation and empowerment. In the tradition of the Hebrew Scriptures, a prophet acted "as the conscience for the community."[22] The Prophet Muhammad of Islam also served in this role. Mystic-activists are prophets. Martin Luther King Jr. was called the Moses of the twentieth century.

The prophetic voice serves as the conscience of the community in two ways. The first is through denunciation, pointing out what is wrong—"the prophet pronounces an indictment of society denouncing its moral and social evils." The second is through annunciation, pointing toward truth and love—"the prophet proclaims the possibility of a new society, an alternative way to view reality and social relations, an alluring picture of the way things should be." Mystic-activists speak out in both voices.

The act of denunciation engages the prophet in truth telling that is often unwelcome to its hearers. He or she offers "a moral and religious indictment of the patterns of behavior within society or indeed of society itself."[23] Right after the election of Hitler, Bonhoeffer spoke on the radio and denounced the concept of the *Führer*. The prophet "charges society and persons within society with a crime."[24] In his last year of life, Malcolm X was planning to charge the United States at the United Nations with the crime of racism. This was a prophetic denouncement of the United States. Elie Wiesel, a witness of the Nazi Holocaust, denounces the indifference of many to the Holocaust. In his novel *The Town Beyond the Wall*, his character, Michael, declares, "This, was the thing I had wanted to understand ever since the war. Nothing else. How a human being can remain indifferent."[25] Rigoberta Menchú clarifies the prophetic voice of denunciation:

> The work of revolutionary Christians is above all to condemn and denounce the injustices committed against people.... We also denounce the stance of the Church hierarchy because it is so often hand in glove with the government.... That is why I say that the Church in Guatemala is divided in two. The Church of the poor (and many have taken this path) has the same beliefs as the poor. And the Church as a hierarchy, as an institution, is still a little clique.[26]

Denouncement also suggests that "the prophet is not merely interested in reforming social institutions so much as he or she is interested in challenging and transforming the very grounds on which these structures operate."[27] The prophetic words of Rigoberta Menchú exemplify this radical perspective: "We began to understand that the root of all our problems was exploitation. That there were rich and poor and that the rich exploited the poor—our sweat, our labour."[28] Martin Luther King Jr. realized that racism was woven into the heart of culture in the United States. In reference to white superiority, he noted that "White men soon came to forget that the southern social culture and all its institutions had been organized to perpetuate this rationalization."[29]

The second feature of prophetic discourse, annunciation, occurs when "the prophet proclaims the possibility of a new society, an alternative way to view reality and social relations, an alluring picture of the way things should be."[30] Through annunciation, prophets bring *"to public expression those very hopes and yearnings* that have been denied so long and suppressed so deeply that we no longer know they are there."[31] A good example of annunciation was Martin Luther King Jr.'s "I Have a Dream" speech in August 1963. In a section full of announcing possibilities, he proclaimed:

> I have a dream...that one day this nation will rise up and live out the true meaning of its creed—we hold these truths to be self-evident: that all men are created equal. I have a dream that one day on the red hills of Georgia, the sons of former slaves and the sons of former slave-owners will be able to sit down at the table of brotherhood.

> I have a dream that one day, even in the state of Mississippi, a state sweltering with the heat of injustice, sweltering with the heat of oppression, will be transformed into an oasis of freedom and justice. I have a dream that my four children will one day live in a nation where they will not be judged by the color of their skin but by the content of their character. I have a dream today!

> I have a dream that one day, down in Alabama, with its vicious racists, with its governor having his lips dripping with the words of interposition and nullification, that one day, right there in Alabama, little black boys and black girls will be able to join hands with little white boys and white girls as sisters and brothers. I have a dream today!

> I have a dream that one day every valley shall be exalted, every hill and mountain shall be made low, the rough places shall be made plain, and the crooked places shall be made straight, and the glory of the Lord shall be revealed and all flesh shall see it together. This is our hope.[32]

King powerfully announced an "imaginative alternative to a racist society" in the United States.[33] He called for social justice and reconciliation. King even used words from the Hebrew prophet Isaiah when singing out his hope for the future (Isa 40). Prophetic annunciation is central to a revolution of the spirit.

Personal Integrity and Social Ethics

In addition to choices in the social realm, mystic-activists also make choices in their personal lives that positively or negatively affect their life work. Personal and social ethics cannot be divorced. Mystic-activists must take a holistic approach, and a transparent one. They strive to take up the challenge of living personally what they proclaim publicly. This is essential, but not easy.

Malcolm X was aware of the need for consistency between his personal practice and his public life. In an interview he said, "I own nothing, except a record player. I have no material possessions. The house where I am living is owned by the Temple. The clothes I wear are made (sewn) by the Muslim women." Malcolm's stated reason for limiting what he owned, "Frequently a very sincere leader becomes trapped by material possessions and consequently he becomes alienated from the aspirations of his followers."[34] As an advocate for the underprivileged, as well as the racially oppressed, Malcolm X chose to deny many benefits of his leadership status and popularity.

Mystic-activists have something in common with everyone else—they are human, for better or for worse. Although they may believe God calls them, they do not consider themselves perfect humans. They struggle with human frailty. They make decisions that, upon later reflection, turn out to be wrong. Dietrich Bonhoeffer regularly told his seminarians that, given the risks they encountered under the Nazi regime, they should avoid marriage. Then Bonhoeffer rejected his own advice and became engaged. One month later, he was arrested. One could argue that Bonhoeffer's advice to his seminarians was the wisest course of action given the circumstances they lived under. But Dietrich fell in love. He was human.

Mystic-activists often face choices that rip and tear their lives and the lives of those they love. Malcolm X and Aung San Suu Kyi both sacrificed relationships with their families for the cause.[35] Malcolm X traveled extensively, speaking and starting mosques. In the last year of his life, he was out of the country a majority of the time, and when he was in the United States he was on the lecture circuit. This meant that Betty Shabazz operated as a single parent much of the time, even before Malcolm X's death. Aung San Suu Kyi chose the liberation of her people in Burma over living with her family. She could have left Burma at any time to rejoin her family in England. Suu Kyi chose to remain in Burma, knowing that the military junta would never allow her to return if she left. This decision meant that Michael Aris was a single parent and died without his life partner at his side. Some would argue that the sacrifice of family is too high of a cost. Bonhoeffer wrote that God's call is costly.

Sometimes it seems as though activists are married to a movement for social justice. Civil rights activist Stokely Carmichael revealed in his autobiography: "Unfortunately I was incapable of giving my energies equally to both the revolution and the family. One had to be sacrificed, and in my case, that ended up being the family. I wish it could have been otherwise, but struggle demands a price. For most people, rightly so, family is the most important thing. For revolutionaries, family often has to be sacrificed to struggle." Carmichael further reflected, "I made my choices. Anytime I chose, I could have chosen family, sought financial security, and abandoned revolution. I don't regret the choice. What I do regret is that my wives had to suffer for my political activities."[36]

Ethical choices are often complex and messy. Mystic-activists face the very human dilemma of living with difficult choices. Pacifist Dietrich Bonhoeffer's decision to join a conspiracy to assassinate Adolf Hitler has troubled many. Did he betray a core belief of his faith? Did he show a lack of integrity? Others argue that Bonhoeffer made a morally correct choice. Knowing of the evil of Hitler, Bonhoeffer believed that not intervening in the Nazi genocide of Jews would have been unethical and morally reprehensible.

Sometimes ethical expectations differ due to cultural contexts. Both Martin Luther King Jr. and Rigoberta Menchú were challenged in their scholarship. King was accused of plagiarism in his graduate work. The accuracy of Menchú's first autobiography, *I, Rigoberta Menchú: An Indian Woman in Guatemala*, has been questioned. King and Menchú both are from oral cultures where the rules are very different than academic or journalistic standards. King's documentation in his university work was sloppy or often missing. The oral culture does not require that one credit a source. In the oral culture of the preachers that influenced King, the Gospel belongs to God and is therefore the shared property of the community. Preachers often preach each other's sermons without giving credit to the source. Menchú shared stories about brutality and persecution in Guatemala, some of which a scholar said never occurred to her family members.[37] As she opens her book, she states that she is writing the story of all Guatemalans.[38] Perhaps she tells the story of her people in the first person. Given that King and Menchú wrote for audiences that use a set of rules that differs from oral culture, perhaps they should have been more careful.

Mystic-activists undergo risk and suffering in many forms. Misinformation and character assassination are forms of persecution used to discredit them. Aung San Suu Kyi reports that the Burmese government has "been trying that all the time with false propaganda about me—all sorts of nonsense. Things like I have four husbands, three husbands, two husbands. That I am a communist—although in some circles they say I am CIA. They have been trying to get prominent monks to say I have been insulting the Buddha."[39] Bonhoeffer, Malcolm X, and Suu Kyi were all under surveillance. Because of heightened scrutiny of public figures and religious leaders, the rumors of Martin Luther King Jr.'s extramarital affairs and Gandhi's tests of his celibacy vow might have damaged seriously their credibility as moral leaders if they had lived in the twenty-first century.

Some mystic-activists experience imprisonment. Others endure physical beatings or torture. Willingness to risk their lives for the cause they believe in, the people they hope to liberate, and the God they serve distinguishes some mystic-activists. Some will join the ranks of martyrs.

Besides external pressures, all mystic-activists have the potential for self-destruction. One who compromises her or his integrity by falling prey to power needs, ego desires, financial rewards, sexual temptations, drug and alcohol abuse, or other such things potentially limits or damages the cause. The stress that comes from taking the path of the mystic-activist makes one even more vulnerable.

Dietrich Bonhoeffer "emerges from his writings as a person who, despite his personal flaws, was led by a deep, prayerful faith to undertake great risks to his life in working for the restoration of justice in a society befouled by systemic immorality."[40] This can also be said of

Malcolm X and Aung San Suu Kyi and rings true of the lives of other activists mentioned in this book.

A Socially Just Society

Aimé Césaire wrote in *Discourse on Colonialism*: "A civilization that proves incapable of solving the problems it creates is a decadent civilization. A civilization that chooses to close its eyes to its most crucial problems is a stricken civilization. A civilization that uses its principles for trickery and deceit is a dying civilization."[41] Mystic-activists are prophets who seek to open eyes to see the exploitative political and social systems in their societies. They prophesy to dying societies. They announce, they call for, a revolution of the spirit in order to create a more just and humane system. They plead for social systems that breathe life into communities.

Similar to Césaire, Howard Thurman declared:

> If there be any government or social institution of whatever kind that operates among people in a manner that makes for human misery, whether of the mind through fear and despair, or of the body through the freezing of the freedom of movement, or of the spirit through the destruction of any sense of the future, such a government or such a social institution, without regard to its sanctions, is evil.

Then Thurman sounded this warning: "To the extent that it is so, it cannot survive, because it is against life and carries within the seeds of its own destruction. The moral law is binding. There is no escape."[42] The cry for a revolution of the spirit emerges because an unjust society by its nature is a dying civilization.

Many twentieth-century mystic-activists did not have the opportunity to participate in the creation of a new and just government. Dietrich Bonhoeffer returned to Germany from the United States so that he might join such an effort but was executed before the war ended. Malcolm X was murdered as he was moving into a phase of life that held great promise for social change. Aung San Suu Kyi's political party was elected so that she might help construct a socially just government. The military dictatorship has not recognized the election as valid.

While these mystic-activists do not present a detailed blueprint for a new government or a just society, they do point toward some of the needed ingredients. Revolution implies that something new needs to be created. A new kind of community, nation, and society needs to be built on a foundation of integrity. Aung San Suu Kyi states, "Political integrity means just plain honesty in politics. One of the most important things is never to deceive the people. Any politician who deceives the people either for the sake of his party or because he imagines it's for the sake of the people, is lacking in political integrity."[43]

In order to reach a place of integrity, confession or truth telling is often required. Catholic monk and social critic Thomas Merton wrote that if whites in the United States listen to the truth told by African Americans "the whites may have to admit that *their prosperity is rooted to some extent in injustice and in sin.*" Merton further stated that such a confession "might lead to a complete reexamination of the political motives behind all our current policies, domestic and foreign, with the possible admission that we are wrong. Such an admission might, in fact, be so disastrous that its effects would dislocate our whole economy and ruin the country."[44] While at first glance Merton's vision appears somewhat naïve, it also seems refreshing and, if ever embraced by a dominant group in a society, courageous and transformative.

In addition to integrity, a new order is built on justice. Aung San Suu Kyi notes, "The Buddhist concept of law is based on *dhamma,* righteousness or virtue, not on the power to impose harsh and inflexible rules on a defenceless people. The true measure of the justice of a system is the amount of protection it guarantees to the weakest. When there is no justice there can be no secure peace."[45] Mohandas Gandhi insisted that "improving the conditions of the most oppressed [was] the decisive test of political sincerity."[46] Liberation ethics implies that the test of a society's commitment to social justice is its treatment of those at the margins.

Since 1994, South Africa has been in the process of nation building. Efforts have been made to develop a just government to replace the previous unjust and corrupt apartheid government. The hope is to build a society on the foundations of reconciliation and social justice. This requires an ongoing revolution of the spirit. Allan Boesak writes that such revolution is only possible by "standing where God stands, however, sharing the pain and the destitution of the poor, feeling the pain of their exclusion as well as the burning for their right to inclusion." The success of the venture cannot be assessed "from the comfortable seats of power, but from the depths of the pits from where the poor are yearning to be heard. Reconciliation begins truly when the voice from the pit is heard, and when that voice sets the tone. For that is the voice that unmasks the lie, reveals the truth, disempowers the myth, opens the way."[47] Government should be judged by "its response to the poor and weak of our society, in terms of its laws, economic policies, social and political transformation; it all must be measured through the eye that looks from the pit." A revolution of the spirit is complete when the poor, excluded, and exploited in a society are content. They have "seen and found justice so that their human potential stands a chance of fulfillment."[48]

In his final days, Dietrich Bonhoeffer contemplated "forgiveness within history" as a feature of a society built on justice. From prison he mused,

> This forgiveness within history can come only when the wound of guilt is healed, when violence has become justice, lawlessness has become order, and war has become peace. If this is not achieved, if wrong still rules unhindered and still inflicts new wounds, then, of course, there can be no question of this kind of forgiveness and man's first concern must be to resist injustice and to call the offenders to account for their guilt.[49]

Bonhoeffer did not live to see this actualized in history. Perhaps he foresaw the spirit of something envisioned in truth and reconciliation commissions in South Africa and elsewhere.

The spirit of prophecy shapes the ethics of the revolution. The authenticity of any new society is built on the foundation of the ethics of that revolution. Aung San Suu Kyi declares, "The quintessential revolution is that of the spirit, born of an intellectual conviction of the need for change in those mental attitudes and values which shape the course of a nation's development.... Without a revolution of the spirit, the forces which produced the iniquities of the old order would continue to be operative, posing a constant threat to the process of reform and regeneration."[50]

9
A LIVED FAITH

In the summer of 1962, a forty-four-year-old African American woman who had spent her entire life working on a cotton plantation in Ruleville, Mississippi, much like her parents and enslaved grandparents, felt her "longing for justice...charged by new moral and spiritual energies."[1] Fannie Lou Hamer attended a civil rights rally for the first time in her life and responded to a call to go to the county courthouse to register to vote—something unheard of for African Americans in the apartheid-like State of Mississippi. Hamer caught a glimpse of a future free from segregation and poverty at that rally. The next day, she traveled with a group of African Americans to register to vote. Hamer led the group off of the bus and into the courthouse. She was one of two individuals the officials allowed to fill out an application. Fannie Lou Hamer did not pass the literacy test that asked her to interpret Mississippi's state constitution. Typically only African Americans were required to pass such tests. Therefore, she was not allowed to register. What seemed like a small gesture, her attempt to register to vote, forever changed Hamer's daily life. She was immediately fired from her job and forced to move to a new residence. A few days later, white supremacists tried to kill her.

Fannie Lou Hamer finally registered to vote, at which point her husband was also dismissed from his job on the plantation. Living in poverty, yet committed to civil rights, she kept up the struggle for change. Hamer attended a training event for civil rights workers held in a nearby state in the summer of 1963. On the return trip, the bus stopped in Winona, Mississippi, where Winona police officers arrested Hamer and several other civil rights activists. The police tortured and brutalized the activists. When the white officers came for Hamer, they recognized her as the woman who had been challenging segregation in Mississippi. So they began to verbally assault her. Two African American male inmates were brought in to physically beat Hamer. Some of the white policeman also joined in. By the time they had finished battering Fannie Lou Hamer, "one of her kidneys was permanently damaged, and a blood clot that formed over her left eye threatened her vision."[2] Hamer was returned to her jail cell and "left alone to bear the physical and spiritual effects of torture."[3]

The next morning, Fannie Lou Hamer's deeply held faith emerged in dramatic fashion. She began to sing. She reflected later, "When you're in a brick cell, locked up, and haven't done anything to anybody but still you're locked up there, well sometimes words just begin to come to you and you begin to sing."[4] So Hamer sang an old spiritual, "Paul and Silas was bound in jail, let my people go." She said, "Singing brings out the soul."[5] Soon, the other civil rights workers in the jail joined her in song. Hamer exclaimed, "It wouldn't solve any problem for me to hate whites just because they hate me."[6] Her response can only be understood in the realm of the spirit. During the next few days, Hamer witnessed to the power of her reconciling faith in encounters with the white jailer and his wife. They were disarmed by her truthful words and loving spirit.

The faith of Fannie Lou Hamer transformed the hour of her most traumatic experience into an amazing decade and a half of leadership in the Civil Rights Movement. Hamer exuded a living faith. It was not enough just to say that you were a Christian, she said. "If you are not putting that claim to the test, where the rubber meets the road, then it's high time to stop talking about being a Christian," declared Hamer. "You can pray until you faint, but if you're not gonna get up and do something, God is not gonna put it in your lap."[7]

The story of Fannie Lou Hamer adds yet another witness to the spirituality of mystic-activists. Mystic-activists *live* their faith. The white supremacists who tortured and harassed Hamer claimed to be religious. There were Nazi leaders in Germany who imprisoned and executed Dietrich Bonhoeffer who claimed to be Christian. The military dictators in Burma who persecute Aung San Suu Kyi claim to be Buddhist. Mystic-activists live out a claim that God makes on their lives.

The hypocrisy of faith in the institutional church in Germany led Dietrich Bonhoeffer, in his prison cell, to contemplate a religionless Christianity. He called for a faith lived in the world of real life and not just inside the four walls of a church. Religionless Christianity was a faith of action and not just ritual. The church in Germany was so corrupt and polluted that it had lost its authenticity. Bonhoeffer believed that the only form of spirituality that could assert some integrity was that which was *lived* in prayer and action—*lived* in a quiet contemplative relationship with God, and *lived* in an aggressive activism that pursued God's mandate for social justice and reconciliation.

This *lived* faith is a hallmark of the leadership of mystic-activists. As mystics, they experience God in direct life-refreshing ways through peak experiences and spiritual practices such as prayer, meditation, and fasting. As activists, they engage directly with societies plagued by injustice, offering prophetic life-giving messages of hope and actions for social change. A *lived* faith is essential for the development of faith-inspired activists in the twenty-first century. In many corners of the world, religious faith has been compromised and disregarded because of religious endorsement of nationalism, terrorism, genocide, ethnic cleansing, materialism, escapist tendencies, elitism, sexism, racism, homophobia, and the like. The world of the twenty-first century needs followers of a religionless faith—a faith of action, not just rituals and rules.

The *lived* faith of mystic-activists gives birth to unique worldviews, identities, and ethics. These interpretations, rooted in the deepest aspects of faith, compel faith-inspired activists to reach for authenticity in their leadership and propel them to struggle for a society that aligns with the vision for social justice in their Scriptures.

The twenty-first century offers complex challenges that require the ability to view life through a multiplicity of lenses. The activists of the new generation can gain much from embracing a worldview in solidarity with the margins. The twenty-first century finds the world feeling like a smaller place shared by more people. Conflict related to diversity is taking center stage. Therefore, leaders need to embrace an identity rooted in humanity. An ethics of revolution is required in order to pursue a faith-inspired vision of social justice and reconciliation. The revolution of the spirit is far from finished. It remains a dynamic call for the twenty-first century.

The *lived* faith narratives of Dietrich Bonhoeffer, Malcolm X, Aung San Suu Kyi, and other mystic-activists suggest ways to empower a new generation in the twenty-first century. It is easy to be overwhelmed by the lives in this book. Their stories are written with bold strokes across the canvas of history. Their human failings as well as their successes offer lessons to social justice leaders of the twenty-first century. The tensions between family relationships and commitment to the cause also face activists in this century. Personal ethics and social responsibility cannot be separated without consequences. Some of what the mystic-activists in this book accomplished was defined and determined by the context in which they lived. Our times and social contexts may be very different. Yet, the way they lived in their times can inform how we live in our times. We can look to them as sisters and brothers in the struggle—even as mentors to guide our journeys of faith and activism.

What do their lives of faith say to us? I want to consider again the faith of mystic-activists. Faith-inspired activists live and practice their faith in ways that do not recognize socially constructed boundaries They strive to transcend race, culture, class, and other artificial limitations. Mystic-activists do not divorce faith from political action for social justice; they do not separate present reality from a hopeful vision for the future; and they view the boundaries of religions as permeable.

Faith and Political Action

Some religious leaders teach their followers not to engage in efforts to create social change. Mytic-activists do not follow this teaching. Some governments also restrict political dissent. The government in Burma placed Aung San Suu Kyi under house arrest during the elections in 1990 for this reason. Equally troubling are societies that co-opt religion to serve the nation. Religious nationalism occurs when a political party or policy position is wedded to a religious institution or belief system. This happened in Germany when church leaders were seduced into an alliance with the Nazi party. Mystic-activists, like the Hebrew prophets, speak truth to politics. They do not willingly allow theological premises or government restrictions to quiet their voices. Nor do they become the puppet of any government. They speak the truth out of their Scripture and faith tradition and seek "to erase the distinction between a *mystic* internal and a political *external*."[8]

Mohandas Gandhi addressed the notion of separating faith from political action: "I can say without the slightest hesitation, and yet in all humility, that those who say that religion has nothing to do with politics do not know what religion means."[9] Rabbi Abraham Heschel spoke out against the United States military involvement in Vietnam during the 1960s and 1970s. "To speak of God and remain silent on Vietnam is blasphemous."[10] After marching with Martin Luther King Jr. in the Selma to Montgomery civil rights march, Heschel exclaimed, "I felt my legs were praying."[11] Martin Luther King Jr. declared, "Any religion that professes to be concerned about the souls of men and is not concerned about the slums that damn them, the economic conditions that strangle them, and the social conditions that cripple them is a spiritually moribund religion awaiting burial."[12]

Dietrich Bonhoeffer did not divorce his faith from action for social justice. He considered the two inseparable. While reflecting on the condition of Nazi-ruled Germany during his final days in prison, he wrote: "Our being Christians today will be limited to two things: prayer and action for justice on behalf of all people. All Christian thinking, speaking, and organizing must be born anew out of this prayer and action."[13] Only a lived faith could claim authenticity after the institutional church had sold its soul to Nazi nationalism.

For Malcolm X, faith was only worth embracing if it promoted social justice for African Americans. "There is no religion under the sun that would make me forget the suffering that Negro people have undergone in this country.... So whether I'm Muslim, Christian, Buddhist, Hindu, atheist or agnostic, I would still be in the front lines with Negro people fighting against the racism, segregation, and discrimination practiced in this country at all levels in the North, South, East, and West."[14] After his conversion to orthodox Islam, Malcolm X began to work for the liberation of all humanity, especially in race relations.

He believed that racial divisions could be resolved through Islam. "The religion of Islam absolutely eliminates racism...it's the only spiritual force that has the sufficient strength to eliminate racism from the heart of the person. So that when a Muslim, *a true Muslim, who practices the religion of Islam* as it was taught by the prophet Muhammad, who was born and died in Arabia some fourteen centuries ago, *a true Muslim* never looks at a person and sees him just by the color of his skin."[15] He believed that Islam could "remove the 'cancer of racism' from the heart of the white American."[16] For Malcolm X, faith was the only hope for addressing racial injustice. He began with the notion that faith was useless without action. As he practiced his faith, he also embraced the corollary that action was fruitless without faith.

Aung San Suu Kyi found that her faith empowered her to engage in political action for social justice. "After all, the Buddha did not accept the status quo without questioning it."[17] Suu Kyi understood Buddhism as an activist faith. "I remind the people that *karma* is actually doing. It's not just sitting back. Some people think of *karma* as destiny or fate and that there's nothing they can do about it.... But *karma* is not that at all. It's doing, it's action. So you are creating your own *karma* all the time. Buddhism is a very dynamic philosophy and it's a great pity that some people forget that aspect of our religion."[18]

A journalist asked Suu Kyi why she spoke of religion in her speeches. She answered, "Because politics is about people, and you can't separate people from their spiritual values." The journalist then asked a student who was in the audience at one of Aung San Suu Kyi's political speeches, "Why are they talking about religion?" To which the student replied, "Well, that's politics."[19]

A Hopeful Vision Rooted in Reality

Dietrich Bonhoeffer, Malcolm X, and Aung San Suu Kyi committed their lives to change the structures of domination. They did not accept injustice or the status quo as inevitable. They recognized the interrelationship between contemplation that seeks inner serenity and a vision of hope that longs for a socially just world. Devotion to Scripture and spiritual practices gives birth to a vision of hope.

Elie Wiesel spoke of hope after surviving the Jewish Holocaust, which killed his family. He claims, "For the religious person, hope is a divine gift. Born in the most obscure realm of one's being, it blossoms only at the paradoxical moment when its absence is stronger than its presence. Hope against hope means I hope because I have no choice—because I am hopeless."[20] When hope comes as a gift, it is a gift we must choose to embrace. We must have the outrageous audacity to reject despair and choose hope. Hope allows "us to go beyond our limits and project ourselves into an uncertain future where dream and desire have the force of memory. Thus one may say that the human being is defined by his or her hope."[21]

As a seasoned mystic, Howard Thurman wrote, "It is not possible to keep the consciousness of the presence of God" fresh and real "over long time intervals." Yet the mystical experience "leaves a deposit in [one's] personality."[22] Martin Luther King Jr. experienced this deposit in his personality when he proclaimed, "In the midst of outer dangers I have felt an inner calm and known resources of strength that only God could give. In many instances I have felt the power of God transforming the fatigue of despair into the buoyancy of hope."[23]

Aung San Suu Kyi was asked if she could actually picture the leaders of the military dictatorship sitting in her house discussing reconciliation. She replied with a smile, "Oh, very much so. I have no trouble envisaging such a thing. That might just be wishful thinking, in some people's interpretation, but it will have to happen some day. I don't know who will be involved, but it will happen."[24] Mystic-activists clearly recognize that faith produces a quality of hope that infuses them with a compelling vision of a just future. There is no boundary separating present reality from the future possibility.

Dietrich Bonhoeffer expressed this need for hopeful vision in the midst of the hopelessness of a Nazi dictatorship: "One may ask whether there have ever before in human history been people with so little ground under their feet—people to whom every available alternative seemed equally intolerable, repugnant, and futile, who looked beyond all these existing alternatives for the source of their strength so entirely in the past or in the future, and who yet, without being dreamers, were able to await the success of their cause so quietly and confidently."[25] Then Bonhoeffer cried out: "Who stands fast? Only the man whose final standard is not his reason, his principles, his conscience, his freedom, or his virtue, but who is ready to sacrifice all this when called to obedient and responsible action in faith and in exclusive allegiance to God—the responsible man, who tries to make his whole life an answer to the question and call of God. Where are these responsible people?"[26] A lonely Dietrich Bonhoeffer was pleading for more people to choose hope and walk the path of mystic-activism. His earnest plea travels across time and rings with the same sense of urgency today.

Interfaith Intersections

Many traditional mystics do not recognize religious boundaries. Sufi scholar Seyyed Hossien Nagr writes, "Every authentic spirituality has its distinct perfume which is an extension of the perfume of paradise and reflects the celestial archetype that is the primal reality of the spirituality in question."[27] Mystics experience the divine presence within a realm that is spiritual and not institutional. For Howard Thurman, "the goal of the mystic, therefore, is to know God in a comprehensive sense; for God is grasped by the whole self or the whole self is laid hold upon by God—the vision of God is realized inclusively."[28] Mystics seek to know God as God—not limited by the narrow interpretive lens of Hinduism, Judaism, Christianity, Buddhism, Islam, or any other religion. While deeply rooted in their own faith tradition, contemplatives rarely feel bound by a religious tradition when seeking union with the divine.

Many mystic-activists perceive and practice their faith like traditional contemplatives. Mohandas Gandhi wrote, "When I was turning over the pages of the sacred books of different faiths for my own satisfaction I became sufficiently familiar for my own purpose with Christianity, Islam, Zoroastrianism, Judaism and Hinduism. In reading these texts, I can say that I was equiminded towards all these faiths [and] read each sacred book in a spirit of reverence, and found the same fundamental morality in each."[29]

Faith-inspired activists often find inspiration in other faith traditions or from the lives of social justice activists of other religions.

Darrell J. Fasching and Dell Dechant called this phenomenon "passing over and coming back."[30] They illustrate this with the examples of Mohandas Gandhi and Martin Luther King Jr.:

> Gandhi's ethical views were shaped not only his own Hinduism but by Tolstoy's writings on Jesus' Sermon on the Mount, and King's ethical views were deeply shaped by Gandhi's insights into the Hindu scripture the *Bhagavad Gita*. Gandhi did not become a Christian and King did not become a Hindu, but in each case their own religious identity was deeply influenced by the other. Martin Luther King, Jr. was a different kind of Christian because of Gandhi and Gandhi was a different kind of Hindu because of Tolstoy.[31]

Aung San Suu Kyi's commitment to nonviolence was deeply shaped by both Gandhi and King. She did not become a Hindu or a Christian. Yet as Fasching and Dechant might say, Suu Kyi was a different kind of Buddhist because of Gandhi and King. Similarly, Dietrich Bonhoeffer was a different kind of Christian because he began to view life through the eyes of Jews in Germany. He read the Hebrew Scriptures with a Jewish lens and recognized the Jewish ethnicity of Jesus.

In addition to the influence of other religious traditions, some develop relational ties with mystic-activists rooted in other faith traditions. In the last year of his life, Malcolm X was reaching out to Martin Luther King Jr. An alliance between the Muslim cleric and the Christian preacher could have been powerful. The Dalai Lama values his encounters with Catholic monk Thomas Merton. In a dramatic "passing over and coming back" in the realm of spiritual practice, Father Daniel Berrigan, a Christian protesting against the war in Vietnam in the 1960s, shared the Eucharist with Vietnamese Buddhist Thich Nhat Hanh. Also Nhat Hanh recited a reading from the Heart Sutra. Interestingly, this took place on the day that Martin Luther King Jr. was assassinated. Faith-based social justice activists often discover they have "more in common with deeply spiritual persons in other traditions than with many in one's own."[32]

Mystic-activists are usually grounded firmly in the richness of their own spiritual traditions. They experience conversions and practice prayer, meditation, fasting, and other spiritual disciplines all within their particular religious tradition. Yet when they plumb the depths of their faith, they reemerge with an amazingly similar *lived* faith based on the deepest meanings found in their separate religious traditions. Their mystic faith protects them from the allure of narrow-minded and isolated viewpoints and implants a hunger for God's peace and justice and for the unity of the human family.

Faith-inspired social activist leaders of the twenty-first century need to discover in their faith the capacity to balance the political and contemplative. Their spiritual practices will lead them to the surprising experience of hope when faced with what seems like overwhelming odds. Twenty-first-century mystic-activists need not fear interactions with mystic-activists from other faith traditions. More so than their twentieth-century mentors, mystic-activists of the twenty-first century must increase their efforts to develop interfaith relationships and alliances because they will be called to work for reconciliation in a time when much of the divisive turmoil includes a religious dimension.

Rest in the Midst of Activism

Fannie Lou Hamer died in 1977 at the age of fifty-nine, the result of diabetes, cancer, stress, and the lack of quality health care for African Americans in Mississippi. Theologian Barbara A. Holmes recounts going to a conference where a friend and coworker of Hamer spoke about the life of the late civil rights activist. That evening, Holmes sat with Hamer's husband and the speaker of the day, Victoria Gray Adams. Holmes asked, "Why did Fannie Lou Hamer die so young?" Adams replied, "If it had not been for the Civil Rights Movement she would have died sooner." Hamer was not physically well for much of her life, and she daily faced the unmerciful forces of racism and poverty. Adams noted, "Her back hurt and her spirit waged war without proper food or medicine. So when the movement came, there was rest." Holmes reflects on Adam's insight into Hamer's spirituality: "This is a rest that wafts from a wellspring of intentional justice-seeking as spiritual practice.... Fannie Lou Hamer was cloistered in an activist environment, finding her focus, restoration, and life in God in the midst of the beloved community already here and yet coming."[33]

Fannie Lou Hamer was a mystic-activist. She was rooted in her Scriptures and the experiential side of her faith tradition. In their conversation about Hamer, Holmes and Adams add another dimension to our understanding of the faith experience of mystic-activists. The struggle for justice itself creates a space for contemplative rest. Activism in the cause of liberation opens up a place of mystical tranquility in the midst of hostility. For mystic-activists, individual and systemic racism, sexism, classism, and other forms of injustice are spiritual issues. Therefore, activism against injustice is a spiritual discipline. Mystic-activists learn "that courage deepens the silences, that putting one's body on the line for another can be a form of prayer, and that shared risk, like shared suffering, teaches us forms of humility, love, and compassion that are often too deep for words."[34] Through spiritual practices, the activist finds renewal. So as Holmes and Adams noted, Hamer extended her life because she found a psychic and spiritual rest in the midst of the spiritual practice of struggling for social justice and reconciliation.

Aung San Suu Kyi regards Buddhism "not just as an inherited religion, but as a living faith."[35] Thich Nhat Hanh describes Buddhism in a way that resonates with Suu Kyi's faith. "Our faith must be alive.... Faith implies practice, living our daily life in mindfulness. Some people think that prayer or meditation involves only our minds or our hearts. But we also have to pray with our bodies, with our actions in the world. And our actions must be modeled after those of the living Buddha or the living Christ."[36] When Suu Kyi faced guns pointed at her with the intent to kill and she just walked on past the soldiers holding those guns, she lived her faith. Her body prayed. Every time she defies the military junta in protests and rallies, she rests in a momentary experience of the freedom she longs for in her struggle for a revolution of the spirit. Activism is a spiritual practice.

In their dialogue on Fannie Lou Hamer, Holmes and Adams spoke of a place of rest for the mystic-activist who personally faced injustice. Hamer experienced the daily bruises of racism. Her leadership in the Civil Rights Movement offered a hope for the future, a present experience of community, and therefore a respite from oppression. When Malcolm X and Aung San Suu Kyi challenged oppression, they experienced a brief break from the trauma of injustice imposed on them. What about mystic-activists, like Dietrich Bonhoeffer, who emerge from locations of power and privilege? Do they also experience a sense of contemplative rest in the midst of fighting injustice?

Dietrich Bonhoeffer left Germany for New York City just prior to the outbreak of World War II. He was discouraged by the lack of commitment from many Confessing Church pastors to challenge the anti-Semitism of the Nazi government. He also felt a need for some rest after several years of stressful activism. So he used his privilege to arrange for a break—a sabbatical of sorts—at Union Theological Seminary. When Bonhoeffer arrived in New York, he did not experience rest. Rather, he was overcome by restlessness. Bonhoeffer had so identified with those at the margins that it seems this prophet with a marginalized worldview could not find respite through an act of privilege. So he went right back to Germany and reentered the struggle against injustice where his spiritual rest was waiting. Bonhoeffer's internal peace was found in his work for peace and justice in Germany, not in the quiet safety of the United States.

Mystic-activists are rooted in the study of their Scriptures and in spiritual practices such as meditation, prayer, and fasting. Calling activism a spiritual discipline does not replace the other practices. Dietrich Bonhoeffer spoke of prayer *and* action. Malcolm X faithfully prayed five times a day *and* challenged a racist nation. Aung San Suu Kyi meditated daily *and* protested for freedom and democracy. What they learned was that God also joined them in their activism against injustice with a gift of inward renewal—a divine calm in the midst of the winds of persecution and prejudice.

Mystic-activists are fully human. Sometimes they stay in an activist mode for far too long and burn themselves out. This is why they must live their faith in the context of a spiritual community of people who will hold them accountable and nurture their spirits. They must also develop relational ties with others who understand the unique challenges of leadership in the struggle against injustice.

Martin Luther King Jr. often faced exhaustion and struggled with depression. This was particularly evident in his final year of life.[37] He was faced with the pressures of launching a massive protest movement—the Poor People's Campaign—and an increased number of threats on his life. He experienced insomnia, depression, "a brooding sense" that his days were numbered, and a longing "for silence, for a time to step back, to pray and reflect."[38]

Vincent Harding, Thich Nhat Hanh, and others were in contact with Thomas Merton about holding a spiritual retreat for King before the Poor People's Campaign began. Before King could rest in the much-needed retreat, he was called to Memphis, Tennessee, to encourage African American sanitation workers protesting for more than poverty wages. So Martin Luther King Jr., the weary mystic-activist, eventually had to find God at the margins of Memphis society, during an evening rally, in the midst of a terrible thunderstorm. He took no notes or prepared manuscript to the pulpit and preached himself and the congregation up to the mountaintop for an encounter with the divine. The next day, he was assassinated.

Mystic-activists are not superheroes. They feel pain and experience despondency. Those who are raised in some semblance of privilege and avoided the most brutal scars of oppression oftentimes experience emotions for which those raised with injustice as a constant companion have developed coping skills. Theologian Dorothee Soelle describes this reality in the life of Dorothy Day, "Like every human being who hungers and thirsts for justice and peace, she too experienced phases of utter exhaustion, sadness, and grief. The word despair seems inappropriate, but it cannot be that far removed from what she went through." When these moments of near despair came to Day, she grieved. "In such times, I was told, she would withdraw and cry. For long hours, days at a time, she would not eat but just sit and weep. She never withdrew from the active, struggling life for the poorest of the poor and never ceased to look upon war and preparation for war as a crime against the poor. But she wept." Soelle reflects further, "When I heard this, I understood a bit better what prayer can mean in the midst of defeat, how the spirit consoles humans and leads them into truth, how one thing is not at the expense of another, and where consolation is purchased with the renunciation of truth. That Dorothy Day cried for days means both consolation and the inconsolability at one and the same time."[39]

Mystic-Activists for the Twenty-First Century

We have taken a journey with three primary actors—Dietrich Bonhoeffer, Malcolm X, and Aung San Suu Kyi—and a supporting cast of many other faith-inspired activists. We have observed that mystic-activists *live* their faith. Mystic-activists brought up in oppression learn to sing like Fannie Lou Hamer. Mystic-activists raised in privilege learn to cry like Dorothy Day. Singing and crying become two sides of the same coin when you live life to its fullest.

I hope that mystic-activists in the twenty-first century will make even greater progress in the work of building a just and reconciled society than these mentors from the twentieth century. May the twenty-first century be a time when many more choose mystic-activism and take a journey of faith in the inner regions of the soul and at the outer regions of the society. Twenty-first-century mystic-activists can find God at the margins, because that is where the struggle against injustice is most visible. But they will also discover that God lurks in the shadows of the palaces of power and privilege, waiting for activists to dismantle the very structures that lock society into the evil of institutionalized injustice and separation. Their call to activism must be enriched by a faith that leads to a healing of their own scarred identities and those of others in society. Twenty-first-century faith-inspired activists need a faith in God that offers a vision of a revolution of the spirit.

If emerging leaders in the twenty-first century choose mystic-activism as their way of life, then we are in for quite a century. The faith of these mystic-activists will unfold in revolutionary action. They will do everything intensely and embrace life with a wide-awake engagement that does not miss much. They are fully committed. They take risks. Their action is rooted in contemplation. Yet they move forward without needing the assurance of knowing the outcome. They live by faith and they live their faith.

EPILOGUE:
RECONCILIATION AND RELIGION
IN THE TWENTY-FIRST CENTURY

In the late 1990s, Muslim and Jewish religious leaders in Palestine and Israel developed a draft of "a first-time-ever treaty or covenant between Judaism and Islam."[1] This occurred quietly out of sight from the official negotiations led by U.S. president Bill Clinton between the political leaders of Israel and the Palestinians. The sheikhs and rabbis envisioned "a parallel track of peacemaking that focused on religion" in the peace process between Palestinians and Israelis.[2] The religious leaders "hoped that the public events surrounding this, and the accompanying symbolism, such as the jolting effect of chief rabbis and sheikhs embracing, would create a religious-psychological breakthrough that would generate its own momentum of peacemaking."[3] Significant progress was made among the religious leaders. Yet when the idea was presented to the politicians leading the official negotiations, the parallel religious process was not implemented. This is an idea that still must become reality in the future if peace is to come to Jerusalem.

For our purposes, the fact that such a reconciliation process found support among religious leaders from both Islam and Judaism is an amazingly hopeful and potentially transformative vision. Similar initiatives are needed around the world in this new millennium. We must pursue reconciliation across the divide of religion. Conflict in the twenty-first century has a religious overlay to it in countless cases. Religious ideology is the source of the tensions in too many situations. Even when religion is not the obvious cause of turmoil, it may sustain the division or fuel the violence. The holy city of Jerusalem—the city whose name speaks of peace—is at the epicenter of a religious fault line where the earthquake of chaos and rage is trembling even as I write this epilogue. Tensions are simmering among Buddhists and Muslims in Thailand. Relations between Hindus, Muslims, and Christians in India still need repair. These few examples represent a rapidly growing global reality. In addition to outright conflict, in most of the world there are limited relational ties among adherents of different faith traditions and significant ignorance of each other's faith histories, beliefs, values, and lifestyles. This lack of interaction means that the stage is set for even more religiously influenced conflicts as cultures increasingly collide in the twenty-first century.

In this brief epilogue, I invite those who seek to link the worlds of social activism and contemplative faith to build more bridges of reconciliation across the chasm of religious division. Moves toward reconciliation embodied and led by everyday faith-inspired activists and religious leaders may be our only hope for greater peace in the world. Reconciliation is "our role in God's script" for the twenty-first century.[4] When people of faith come together in relationship and common purpose for peace, they can inspire people of faith at all levels to build communities of peace.

The Power of Scripture

The power of Scripture must never be underestimated in contexts where people have a faith orientation or religious background. The 1990s peace treaty draft that rabbis and sheikhs developed in the Holy Land used Scripture as a central text for their covenant and for their rationale as peacemakers. The Scriptures of Islam and Judaism exerted moral imperative for the process and anchored the commitment of the participants by engaging their core values. We have seen the centrality of Scripture repeatedly in the formation and empowerment of mystic-activists in the twentieth century. Dietrich Bonhoeffer, Malcolm X, Aung San Suu Kyi, and many others framed their social justice initiatives and human rights movements using the Scriptures and language of their faith traditions.

The biblical word "reconciliation" plays a powerful role in shaping the societal transformation in South Africa. During the transition process in 1993 that led to the national election of Nelson Mandela as president and the end of the apartheid government, leaders discussed the establishment of a truth commission to deal with the crimes of the apartheid era. Allan Boesak describes a critical juncture at these historical negotiations. "Our discussions were interrupted by a request from then President F. W. de Klerk. The National Party was not happy with the term 'truth commission.' It felt strongly that South Africa would be better served if the commission was to be a 'truth *and* reconciliation commission.'" Boesak welcomed this suggestion as a theologian, but warned the team about the implications. "The issue was not reconciliation; it was, rather, our understanding and interpretation of it.... From experience in the church as well as politics we knew how the Bible was used in Afrikaner politics, and how the radical message of the Bible was made servant to ideology, domesticated for purposes of subjection and control.... Mr. de Klerk and his party did not intend to allow reconciliation to confront the country with the demands of the gospel, but to blunt the progress of radical change and transformation."[5]

The politicians around the table all accepted President de Klerk's suggestion. Even those who would soon lead the nation saw value in using the word *reconciliation* for the process. Boesak writes, "They all consciously or unconsciously accepted F. W. de Klerk's subliminal text: adding the word 'reconciliation' would smooth a process fraught with contradictions, risks and danger, loaded as it was with unspeakable things from the past. The religious twist would help tame it, domesticate it, make it more pliable and palatable for the broader public."[6] Boesak recognized their faulty reasoning. "The Scriptures will not be ideologized, manipulated or managed to suit our political endeavors, processes or desires. The demands of the Scriptures will always lay a greater claim than these processes are willing to concede."[7]

The potency of the biblical call to reconciliation enabled the Truth and Reconciliation Commission (TRC) to be a powerful force for unmasking and healing the brutality of apartheid. The word that was calculated to make the process soft and impotent imbued the

Truth and Reconciliation Commission (TRC) with enough theological power to reveal the truth of apartheid's crimes, demand justice, prompt forgiveness, and accelerate a process of healing. As Boesak notes, TRC chair Archbishop Desmond Tutu "could not help himself. The radical nature of the Christian faith and the very reality of biblically motivated reconciliation would often push the TRC into deeper waters than it wanted, or had planned, or could be allowed to go."[8]

"The demands of the Scriptures" mandate and motivate mystic-activists to work for reconciliation and risk their lives for social justice. Scripture lays "a greater claim" on their lives than they can anticipate. Mystic-activists in this century must take the word of reconciliation into the world of religious discord and animosity. Engaging with Scripture for study, interpretation, exhortation, and community application is a primary spiritual discipline of faith communities. Some religious leaders are skilled at this work. Taking this central spiritual endeavor of faith traditions and utilizing it for the pursuit of peace normalizes the work of reconciliation for people of faith. The Scriptures of all major faith traditions speak of peace and social justice.

Bringing texts from various traditions into a comparative study produces interfaith conversation and opens the door to reconciliation. As religious people study each other's texts related to peacemaking, they together begin to share a passion for peace. Joint Scripture study briefly shifts attention from the current struggle toward the eternal demands of peace and justice. This creates "a temporary but sacred time of reconciliation, and temporary suspension of judgment."[9] The reconciliation of present tensions returns to view with a more hopeful outlook as shared understanding turns into deeper relationships.

Scripture study is not just something for the clergy and leaders. Its greatest potential is at the grassroots level in neighborhoods and communities. Rabbi Marc Gopin sees this yielding "new intimacies, such as mutual invitations to homes and meeting with families. This kind of shared study, not for the purposes of debate or conversion, is an innovation in the history of monotheism that will engender a certain kind of healing and reconciliation for many deeply religious people."[10] Something profound happens when people of different faiths sit around the table in homes and community gathering places to study each other's sacred texts. Gopin recommends that for citizens of Israel and Palestine:

> An inter-religious textual study on the sacredness of Jerusalem, a study of all the texts, traditions, metaphors and symbols of all peoples, in a respectful, nonbelligerent atmosphere, may be accomplishing what no dialogue or national bargaining session ever could. This may very well be setting the stage for future coexistence in Jerusalem in a way that no rational bargaining can accomplish right now.... The religious revisioning of sacred spaces can impact the existential orientations of millions of citizens.[11]

Community Building

Developing a sense of community and bonding with other individuals is another spiritual discipline of faith traditions. In order to find reconciliation across religious divides, we need to use our skills at community building in multi-religious contexts. The 1990s religious peace accord process centered in Jerusalem was built on years of quiet relationship-building among some religious leaders who are "not interested in boundaries and borders but relationships and visions"—that is, mystic-activists in the Holy Land.[12] Many of the mystic-activists examined in this book had relationships with social justice activists of other faith traditions. Malcolm X and Martin Luther King Jr. were exploring a relationship at the time of Malcolm's death. The Dalai Lama spent time with Thomas Merton. Daniel Berrigan and Thich Nhat Hanh are friends. Mohandas Gandhi regularly engaged with leaders of other faith traditions. What is true for mystic-activists must become a reality for more and more persons and communities of faith. Relational bonding sustains peacemaking efforts.

Relationship building is the hard work of reconciliation and offers something that cannot be found in social or economic justice initiatives alone. Conflict resolution specialist Mohammed Abu-Nimer calls this "the painful dilemma of reconciliation work—how to work at justice while maintaining or building positive relationships, how to look at the past and correct grievances while creating an amicable and livable present and future for all the protagonists."[13] Relationships rooted in a spiritual bond have great potential for healing and sustaining peace. Reconciliation is a long-term process because, "long after the papers are signed and the handshakes are over, the dismantling of generations of separation, prejudice and violence continues."[14] Networks of interfaith relationships improve the possibility of healing and real friendships emerging.

Worship

Another spiritual discipline of faith traditions is worship. This was a part of wedding the relationships between the sheikhs and rabbis in the late 1990s and nurturing the continuing interfaith reconciliation movement in the Holy Land.[15] A relational bond deepens if we invite each other into our worship of God, opening "a window onto the meaning of the other [and allowing us to] temporarily experience the other's worldview."[16] Words cannot adequately illuminate and support this contention. Worship is experiential and, therefore is its own witness.

Some religious communities and individuals are blending faith traditions. There are Christians who integrate Judaism into their faith practices, such as the observance of the Sabbath and Jewish festivals. They understand Judaism as the mother of Christianity and see the two as one seamless tradition. Some Jews have embraced Jesus as their Messiah, yet remain observant in their Judaism. They sometimes refer to themselves as Messianic Jews. There are Muslims who retain much of their Islamic belief and culture while embracing Jesus as the incarnation of God. These Muslim Christians are sometimes called completed Muslims. Perhaps some Christians accept the prophetic status of Muhammad as equal to Moses. Thich Nhat Hanh is a Buddhist monk who reveres Jesus Christ as a spiritual ancestor alongside the Buddha.[17] And many of different faith backgrounds in the United States practice Buddhist meditation or look to Buddhist teachings to complement their traditions.

I apologize to anyone who finds these terms or concepts offensive. Yet, this pluralistic approach to religious faith illustrates how we can live together in society. We can learn to live with respect and admiration for each other's faith traditions. Though few actually will incorporate each other's practices, we must find reconciliation in the midst of our diverse religious traditions.

A Life of Reconciliation, a World of Reconciliation

Ultimately, spiritual discipline for the individual is about character formation and a transforming experience with God. Marc Gopin believes that if reconciliation becomes the norm in our lives, the life of each one of us has great promise for encouraging peace in our society: "One's character, and the daily internal struggles with anger against others who are different or adversaries, becomes the blueprint of a world that is lived out every day in and through one's struggle to be a bond, to be the glue that bonds the world together."

The idea that an individual person committed to reconciliation can be a "blueprint" of reconciliation or the "glue" that holds opposing sides together is an unnerving, yet exciting, notion. Gopin goes so far as to suggest that one can create "through one's own person, a taste of a future world of peace, justice, respect, and love. That world may only exist, in the interim, inside one's person. But that becomes, and must be recognized as, a unique form of peacemaking that far surpasses dialogue and official programming in terms of spiritual depth."[18]

A challenge for mystic-activists is not only to speak words of reconciliation, but to live lives that communicate the message of reconciliation without a word ever being spoken. The internalization of the character and values of reconciliation precedes authentic activism. Mystic-activists see their lives as "an offering to peace, and therefore to God."[19]

Gopin writes regarding the Holy Land, "If the millions of Jews, Christians, and Muslims who *are* committed in principle to coexistence and compromise actually took the time and developed the skills of reconciliation, the sheer power of their activism, the sheer strength of all their new relationships, would have overwhelmed the political and cultural milieu by now. But they have not because most lack the skills and the courage necessary to engage the stranger, the other who has been an enemy."[20]

I rephrase this in the positive and say, if the millions of people of faith who desire peace and social justice actually take the time to develop relationships with people of other faiths, seek experiences in other faith communities, and acquire the skills needed for peace-making, they will overwhelm the political and cultural milieu. We who are mystic-activists must commit ourselves to embody the blue-print for transformation, serve as the relational glue for reconcilia-tion, and pray without ceasing that our world will encounter and embrace God's peace.

ACKNOWLEDGMENTS

The idea for this book first germinated in the early 1990s. The book began to take concrete shape through the process of writing my doctoral dissertation at the University of St. Thomas in St. Paul, Minnesota. This final form is the result of revisions of the dissertation and fresh additions to the manuscript in consultation with Michael West, senior editor at Fortress Press. So I begin by thanking Fortress Press, and in particular Michael West, Bill Huff, Scott Tunseth, Bob Todd, and Pamela Johnson.

I express my gratitude to the committee that read my doctoral dissertation: Katherine Egan (chair), Bernard Brady, and Friedrich Kustaa. I thank Karen DeYoung for editorial assistance, which significantly improved the quality of the prose. I am grateful for the help of a number of typists during the research phase: Jason Bailey, Lea (Hintermeister) Berg, Sonia Cooper, Rachel DeYoung, Michelle Friesen, Lauren Johnson, and Mercy Olson Ward. The organizations I have worked for during the research and development of this manuscript have been very supportive: Twin Cities Urban Reconciliation Network (TURN), City Gate Project, and Bethel University. Many friends have encouraged me in the process of writing this book. I express my appreciation to Jay Barnes, Allan Boesak, Eldon Fry, Bob and Gayle Holmes, Mark Horst, Bill Huff, James Earl Massey, Claudia May, Chris McNair, Brad McNaught, Aldean Miles, Seth and Merrishia Naicker, Robert Odom, Mercy Olson Ward, Cynthia Read, Karen Ristau, Alroy Trout, and Cecilia Williams.

As always, my wife Karen has given me her full support and love. I am grateful to my activist children, Rachel and Jonathan, who have embraced a strong sense of social justice. I hope this book will encourage them as future leaders. I acknowledge God as the source of all that is good in this book and I pray for the peace, shalom, salaam of Jerusalem.

APPENDIX

Brief Biographical Sketches of Twentieth Century Mystic-Activists

Daniel Berrigan (b. 1921) is a Christian peace activist in the United States involved in nonviolent protests related to civil rights, anti-war, and anti-nuclear weapons issues. He is an ordained Catholic priest and author of several books. He helped found the Plowshares Movement.

Allan Boesak (b. 1946) is a Christian leader who was at the forefront of the antiapartheid movement in South Africa during the 1980s and 1990s, providing leadership for the United Democratic Front—a coalition of churches, labor organizations, student groups, and civic associations. He is an ordained minister in the Uniting Reformed Church and one of the originators of black liberation theology in South Africa.

The Dalai Lama (b. 1935) The fourteenth and current Dalai Lama, Tenzin Gyatso is a Buddhist human rights leader. He leads the Tibetan government-in-exile in India. He is the bodhisattva, or enlightened being, of compassion and the supreme head of Tibetan Buddhism. Through his books, speaking, and meetings with world leaders, he is an advocate for world peace and social justice.

Dorothy Day (1897–1980) was a Christian advocate for the poor and an antiwar activist in the United States. She was a founder of the Catholic Worker Movement. She was known for establishing homes for poor and homeless people in New York City and throughout the country.

Mohandas Gandhi (1869–1948) was a Hindu social justice leader in India, known by his followers as Mahatma, which means "great soul." Trained as a lawyer, Gandhi led nonviolent protest movements in

South Africa and in India. His leadership in India led to the nation's independence from Great Britain.

Fannie Lou Hamer (1917–1977) was a Christian civil rights activist from the United States. She was raised in poverty and joined the struggle for civil rights through voting rights campaigns. Most of her activism focused on conditions for poor African Americans in her home state of Mississippi.

Abraham Joshua Heschel (1907–1972) was a Jewish theologian and civil rights activist born in Poland. He escaped the Nazis, eventually finding his way to the United States. Rabbi Heschel was a professor and an activist.

Martin Luther King Jr. (1929–1968) was a Christian civil rights leader in the United States. He was an ordained Baptist preacher and pastor who emerged as the primary symbol and leader of the Civil Rights Movement in the United States during the 1950s and 1960s.

Winona LaDuke (b. 1959) embraces an indigenous Native American spirituality as an Ojibwe activist in the United States. She focuses on environmental issues and the reclamation of Native American lands, based on the White Earth Indian reservation.

Nelson Mandela (b. 1918) is a Christian and former antiapartheid activist in South Africa who spent 27 years in prison. In 1994 he was elected as the nation's first post-apartheid and first black president.

Rigoberta Menchú (b. 1959) synthesizes indigenous spirituality and Christian Catholicism as a human rights activist in Guatemala. She addresses Indian rights, poverty and labor issues, and cultural reconciliation. She was awarded the 1992 Nobel Peace Prize.

Thomas Merton (1915–1968) was a Catholic monk who bridged traditions between Western and Eastern religions and bridged monasticism and activism.

Thich Nhat Hanh (b. 1926) is a Buddhist peace activist from Vietnam. He was at the forefront of monks protesting against the Vietnam War. He helped found the Unified Buddhist Church and was an originator of "engaged Buddhism," which calls for a spiritual engagement with social action.

Oscar Romero (1917–1980) was a Christian leader for social justice in El Salvador and an archbishop in the Roman Catholic Church. He mobilized the church to address the brutal repression by the government and gave voice to the oppressed and powerless.

Howard Thurman (1900–1981) was a Christian contemplative, theologian, and social critic who served as a professor and pastor. He mentored Martin Luther King Jr. and many others in the Civil Rights Movement.

Desmond Tutu (b. 1931) is a retired archbishop in the Anglican Church and was a leading antiapartheid activist in South Africa. He presided over the Truth and Reconciliation Commission in South Africa and remains active in addressing human rights issues in South Africa and throughout the world.

Elie Wiesel (b. 1928) is a Jewish human rights activist and noted novelist in the United States. Born in Romania, he is a survivor of the Jewish Holocaust of Nazi Germany and his novels are informed by this experience.

NOTES

Full citations to works cited in the Notes section can be found in the Bibliography.

1 Mystic-Activists: An Introduction

1. Garrow, *Bearing the Cross* 57–58. Garrow presented King's sermonic version of this episode. King himself wrote of it in *Stride toward Freedom*, 134–135.

2. Gottlieb, *Joining Hands*, 108.

3. Robert Jay Lifton, *Death in Life* (New York: Basic Books, 1967), 373.

4. *King: A Filmed Record*, prod. and dir. Lumet and Mankiewicz.

5. Lawrence-Lightfoot, "Introduction," xv, and "A View of the Whole," 10.

6. Lawrence-Lightfoot, "Illumination: Navigating Intimacy," 135.

7. Lawrence-Lightfoot, "Illumination: Expressing a Point of View," 86.

8. See DeYoung, *Coming Together*, 186-87 and DeYoung, *Reconciliation*, 137–38.

9. Witcover, *85 Days*, 8.

10. Pollard, *Mysticism and Social Change*, 1, 62. Suzanne Noffke refers to Catherine of Siena as a mystic activist in her introduction to *Catherine of Siena* (9). Barbara A. Holmes uses the term "public mystics" in a similar fashion in *Joy Unspeakable* (152–68). Segundo Galilea calls these leaders "contemplatives in action" in "Liberation as an Encounter with Politics and Contemplation" (25). Complementary themes are discussed in Dorothee Soelle's study of mysticism and resistance, *Silent Cry*.

11. Carmody, *Mysticism*, 10.

12. McGinn, *Foundation of Mysticism*, xvi.

13. Ibid., xvii.

14. Holt, *Thirsty for God*, 70.

15. Nouwen, *Thomas Merton*, 42.

16. Dennis, Golden, and Wright, *Oscar Romero*, 19–20.

17. Baldwin, "Malcolm and Martin," 276.

2 The Just Shall Live by Faith

1. Gottlieb, *Joining Hands*, 9.

2. The Deuteronomy, Isaiah, and Proverbs passages are from *The TANAKH: The New Jewish Publication Society Translation According to the Traditional Hebrew Text* copyright © 1985 by the Jewish Publication Society. Used by permission. The Talmudic passage is from Cohen, *Everyman's Talmud*, 65.

3. The Luke, Galatians, and 1 John passages are from the *New Revised Standard Version*, copyright © 1989 by the Division of Christian Education of the National Council of the Churches of Christ in the USA. Used by permission. All rights reserved.

4. The Qur'an passage from Surah 49 is from Abdullah Yusef Ali, *An English Interpretation of The Holy Qur-an* (Lahore, Pakistan: Sh. Muhammad Ashraf Publishers, 1934). The passages from Surahs 90 and 107 are from Ahmed Ali, *Al-Qur'an: A Contemporary Translation*, Rev. ed. (Princeton: Princeton University Press, 2001).

5. Mohandas K. Gandhi, *The Bhagavad Gita according to Gandhi* (Berkeley: Berkeley Hills Books, 2000).

6. F. Max Müller, trans., *The Dhammapada* (Woodstock, VT: Skylight Paths Publishing, 2002); Sāntideva (Kate Crosby and Andrew Skilton trans.), *The Bodhicaryavatara* (New York: Oxford University Press, 1998).

7. Bonhoeffer, *Discipleship*, 108.

8. Malcolm X, *Malcolm X Speaks*, 61.

9. Menchú, *I, Rigoberta Menchú*, 130.

10. Day, *Long Loneliness*, 166.

11. Bethge, *Dietrich Bonhoeffer*, 202.

12. Bonhoeffer, Letter from Finkenwalde, 27 January 1936, in Bethge, *Dietrich Bonhoeffer*, 204–205.

13. Bonhoeffer, Letter to Karl-Friedrich Bonhoeffer, January 1935, in Bethge, *Dietrich Bonhoeffer*, 205–206.

14. Bonhoeffer, *Discipleship*, 43–56.

15. DeCaro, *Malcolm and the Cross*, 71.

16. Ibid., 83-85, and Collins, *Seventh Child*, 39.

17. Malcolm X, *Autobiography of Malcolm X*, 158.

18. Ibid., 161, 162.

19. Ibid., 172–173.

20. Ibid., 173.

21. Ibid., 346–347.

22. Malcolm X, *The Barry Gray Show*, Station WMCA, New York, July 8, 1964, quoted in Goldman, *Death and Life of Malcolm X*, 166.

23. Thurman, *Mysticism and the Experience of Love*, 5.

24. LaDuke, "Rebuilding Community," 62–63.

25. Jordens, *Gandhi's Religion*, 142.

26. F. Burton Nelson, "Bonhoeffer and the Spiritual Life: Some Reflections," *Journal of Theology for Southern Africa* 30 (March 1980): 36.

27. Paul Lehmann quoted in *I Knew Dietrich Bonhoeffer*, 45.

28. Goldman, *Death and Life of Malcolm X*, 19.

29. Malcolm X, *Speeches at Harvard*, 164.

30. Karim, *Remembering Malcolm*, 166.

31. Hunt, *Future of Peace*, 35.

32. Suu Kyi and Clements, *The Voice of Hope*, 92.

33. Suu Kyi, *Letters from Burma*, 59.

34. Hunt, *Future of Peace*, 35.

35. Suu Kyi, *Letters from Burma*, 199.

36. Murvar, "Integrative and Revolutionary Capabilities of Religion," 75.

3 Dietrich Bonhoeffer: "The View from Below"

1. Bonhoeffer, *Letters & Papers from Prison*, 17.

2. Ibid.

3. Barnes, "Dietrich Bonhoeffer," 111.

4. Bethge, *Dietrich Bonhoeffer*, 19.

5. Bonhoeffer, *Testament to Freedom*, 54.

6. For more details about the ministry of Adam Clayton Powell Sr. and his influence on Bonhoeffer, see Clingan, *Against Cheap Grace*.

7. Bonhoeffer, *No Rusty Swords*, 113.

8. Paul Lehmann, BBC program with E. Bethge, R. Niebuhr, et al., March 13, 1960 (BBC archive LP26507-8), quoted in Bethge, *Dietrich Bonhoeffer*, 155.

9. Bonhoeffer, *Gesammelte Schriften*, 97.

10. Bonhoeffer, *No Rusty Swords*, 112. Bonhoeffer does not identify the poet, but Josiah Young believes this is a reference to Countee Cullen (Young, *No Difference in the Fare*, 123). Cullen's book, *The Black Christ and Other Poems*, was published in 1929, just prior to Bonhoeffer's arrival in the United States.

11. Ibid., 113.

12. Ibid., 113–114.

13. Zimmermann, "Years in Berlin," 64-65.

14. Bonhoeffer, *No Rusty Swords*, 204.

15. Barnes, "Dietrich Bonhoeffer," 111.

16. Ibid.

17. Ibid., 112, 113.

18. Robertson, *Shame and the Sacrifice*, 89.

19. Baranowski, "The Confessing Church," 95.

20. Robertson, *Shame and the Sacrifice*, 93.

21. Bergen, "Storm Troopers of Christ," 50, 51; Heschel, "When Jesus Was an Aryan," 73, 77; Baranowski, "The Confessing Church," 95, 97.

22. Bonhoeffer, *A Testament to Freedom*, 433.

23. Bonhoeffer, *No Rusty Swords*, 229.

24. Ibid., 225.

25. Heinz Eduard Tödt, unpublished manuscript, quoted in Bethge, "Dietrich Bonhoeffer and the Jews," 63.

26. Bonhoeffer also employed the phrase "Negro problem" when writing of race issues in the United States. The term was common in the United States in the 1930s and revealed a similar view that African Americans were the problem, rather than the racism of whites and institutions in the United States.

27. Bethge, *Dietrich Bonhoeffer*, 275–276.

28. Ibid., 607.

29. Kelly and Nelson, *Cost of Moral Leadership*, 17.

30. Bonhoeffer, *A Testament of Freedom*, 412.

31. Baranowski, "The Confessing Church and Antisemitism," 90.

32. Kelly and Nelson, "Solidarity with the Oppressed," 21.

33. Baum, *The Church for Others*, 89.

34. Bethge, *Dietrich Bonhoeffer*, 494.

35. Bonhoeffer, *Testament to Freedom*, 99. See also Kelly and Nelson, *Cost of Moral Leadership*, 103.

36. Kelly and Nelson, *Cost of Moral Leadership*, 104. Originally in Bonhoeffer, *No Rusty Swords*, 188. I prefer the translation by Kelly and Nelson.

37. Wiersma, "Bonhoeffer and Gandhi," 209.

38. Bonhoeffer, *No Rusty Swords*, 290, 291, 292.

39. Kelly and Nelson, *Cost of Moral Leadership*, 210.

40. Kelly and Nelson, "Solidarity with the Oppressed," 33.

41. Bethge, "Dietrich Bonhoeffer and the Jews," 75.

42. Ibid., 74.

43. Erickson and Heschel, "Introduction," 7.

44. Bonhoeffer, *Testament to Freedom*, 493.
45. Bonhoeffer, *Way to Freedom*, 246.
46. Robertson, *Shame and the Sacrifice*, 176.
47. Bethge, *Dietrich Bonhoeffer*, 677.
48. Ibid., 678.
49. Ibid., 677.
50. Ibid., 681.
51. Bethge, "Dietrich Bonhoeffer and the Jews," 76.
52. Bonhoeffer, *Ethics*, 90.
53. Bonhoeffer, *Ethics*, 112. See also Barnes, "Dietrich Bonhoeffer and Hitler's Persecution of the Jews," 126.
54. Ibid., 114. See also Barnes, "Dietrich Bonhoeffer and Hitler's Persecution of the Jews," 127.
55. Bonhoeffer, *Letters & Papers from Prison*, 162.
56. Ibid., 129.
57. Ibid., 16.
58. Bonhoeffer, *Letters & Papers from Prison*, 7.
59. Nelson and Kelly, *Cost of Moral Leadership*, 31.
60. Ibid., 32.
61. Bonhoeffer, *Letters & Papers from Prison*, 279.
62. Kelly, "Prayer and Action for Justice," 250, 251.
63. Bonhoeffer, *Testament of Freedom*, 529.
64. Bonhoeffer, *Letters & Papers from Prison*, 361, 362, 369.
65. Bethge, *Dietrich Bonhoeffer*, 899, 924.
66. Ibid., 920.
67. Ibid., 927.
68. Bonhoeffer, *Discipleship*, 87.
69. Bonhoeffer, Letter from Finkenwalde, 27 January 1936, quoted in Bethge, *Dietrich Bonhoeffer*, 205.

4 A Worldview from the Margins

1. Bonhoeffer, *Letters & Papers in Prison*, 17.
2. Gutiérrez, *Power of the Poor in History*, 231, 233.
3. Malcolm X, Cory United Methodist Church, Cleveland, Ohio, 3 April 1964, quoted in Cone, *Martin & Malcolm & America*, 1.
4. Bianchi, *Religious Experience of Revolutionaries*, 96.
5. Ibid., 18.
6. Daloz, et al., *Common Fire*, 73.
7. Ibid.
8. Menchú, *I, Rigoberta Menchú*, 246.
9. Franklin, *Liberating Visions*, 76.
10. Malcolm X, *Speeches at Harvard*, 135.
11. Sales, *From Civil Rights to Black Liberation*, 207.
12. Ibid., 57.
13. Daloz, et al., *Common Fire*, 76.
14. West, "Malcolm X and Black Rage," 48.
15. Bonhoeffer, *Letters & Papers from Prison*, 17.
16. *La voz de los sin voz* (UCA), March 23, 1980, homily, 291, quoted in Dennis, Golden, and Wright, *Oscar Romero*, 95.

17. Daloz, et al., *Common Fire*, 76.
18. Kelly, *Liberating Faith*, 156.
19. Willie, *Theories of Human Social Action*, 99.
20. Ibid., 105-106.
21. West, *Race Matters*, 43.
22. Daloz, et al., *Common Fire*, 77.
23. Burgos-Debray, "Introduction," xii.
24. King, *I Have a Dream*, 143.
25. Willie, *Theories of Human Social Action*, 100, 107.
26. King, *I Have a Dream*, 95.
27. Sidorenko, *Robert F. Kennedy*, 158
28. Ibid., 156, 158.
29. Ibid., 156, 158-159.
30. Dennis, Golden, and Wright, *Oscar Romero*, 29.
31. Romero, *Voice of the Voiceless*, 138.
32. Dennis, Golden, and Wright, *Oscar Romero*, 30-31.
33. Galilea, "Liberation as an Encounter with Politics and Contemplation," 25.
34. Menchú, *I, Rigoberta Menchú*, 134.
35. De Gruchy, *Bonhoeffer and South Africa*, 83.
36. Day, *Long Loneliness*, 51.
37. Sales, *From Civil Rights to Black Liberation*, 57. Sales notes that many people he knew had met with Malcolm X over meals and other social occasions. "I have been struck by how many people of my generation had meaningful personal encounters with Malcolm X. In an era of media image-making, Malcolm retained the ability to use older more traditional methods to reach and move people.... I would argue that if Malcolm had any particular genius regarding leadership, it was his ability as a public figure to meet so many ordinary people in situations that allowed for some measure of personal interaction" (*From Civil Rights to Black Liberation*, 58).
38. Menchú, *I, Rigoberta Menchú*, 228.
39. Cone, *Black Theology & Black Power*, 99. See also Plant, "Ethics and Materialist Hermeneutics," 108.
40. Harding, *Martin Luther King*, 112–113.
41. Day, *Long Loneliness*, 78.
42. Romero, *Voice of the Voiceless*, 182. See also Kelly and Nelson, *The Cost of Moral Leadership*, 184.
43. Dalai Lama, *Ethics for the New Millennium*, 124.
44. De Gruchy, *Bonhoeffer and South Africa*, 28.
45. Boesak, "What Bonhoeffer Meant to Me," 23.

5 Malcolm X: "Recognizing Every Human Being as a Human Being"

1. Malcolm X, *Malcolm X Speaks*, 35.
2. Ibid., 59.
3. Malcolm X, "Whatever Is Necessary," 186.
4. DeCaro, *On the Side of My People*, 39.
5. Malcolm X, *Autobiography of Malcolm X*, 2, 3.
6. Natambu, *Life and Work of Malcolm X*, 4.
7. Malcolm X, *Autobiography of Malcolm X*, 12.
8. Ibid., 27–28.
9. Ibid., 32–33.

10. Ibid., 37–38.

11. Ibid., 34.

12. Ibid., 44–45.

13. Goldman, *Death and Life of Malcolm X*, 34.

14. Malcolm X, *Autobiography of Malcolm X*, 182.

15. Ibid., 187.

16. Ibid., 193–194.

17. Karim, *Remembering Malcolm*, 25.

18. Ibid., 86.

19. Malcolm X, undated letter to Bazely Perry, quoted in Perry, *Malcolm*, 120.

20. Natambu, *Life and Work of Malcolm X*, 161.

21. Malcolm X, *Autobiography of Malcolm X*, 238.

22. DeCaro, *On the Side of My People*, 113.

23. Goldman, *Death and Life of Malcolm X*, 59.

24. Karim, "Introduction," 4.

25. Goldman, *Death and Life of Malcolm X*, 47.

26. Lincoln, *Black Muslims in America*, 69–70.

27. Malcolm X, *End of White World Supremacy*, 79–80.

28. Carmichael, *Ready for Revolution*, 257.

29. Ibid., 260.

30. Ibid., 259-260.

31. Karim, *Remembering Malcolm,* 138.

32. Cone, *Martin & Malcolm & America*, 183.

33. Malcolm X, *Autobiography of Malcolm X*, 325.

34. Malcolm X on *The Ben Hunter Show* (Los Angeles: Channel 11, 29–30 March 1963), quoted in DeCaro, *On the Side of My People*, 159.

35. Malcolm X, *Autobiography of Malcolm X*, 300–301.

36. Ibid., 312–313.

37. DeCaro, *On the Side of My People*, 190.

38. Wilfred Little, interviewed by Karl Evanzz, quoted in Evanzz, *The Messenger*, 261.

39. Goldman, *Death and Life of Malcolm X,* 136.

40. Malcolm X, *February 1965*, 173.

41. Malcolm X, *Two Speeches*, 5.

42. Al-Hadid, "Al-Qur'an and Sunnah," 74.

43. Malcolm X, *Autobiography of Malcolm X*, 372.

44. Ibid., 373.

45. Ibid., 330, 340.

46. Ibid., 369.

47. Ibid., 382.

48. DeCaro, *On the Side of My People*, 241, 242.

49. Malcolm X, press conference, 21 May 1964, quoted in Wolfenstein, *Victims of Democracy*, 310.

50. Goldman, *Death and Life of Malcolm X,* 226.

51. Ibid., 172.

52. Malcolm X, *Malcolm X Talks to Young People*, 11.

53. Malcolm X, *By Any Means Necessary*, 56.

54. Sales, *From Civil Rights to Black Liberation*, vii, viii.

55. For more details see Evanzz, *The Judas Factor*, 226ff. This may be the only time they met face to face. Also see Collins, *Seventh Child*, 99. Rodnell Collins, Malcolm's

nephew (son of his half sister Ella), wrote that when Malcolm X opened the first temple in Boston of the Nation of Islam "in 1952/1953 at 405 Massachusetts Avenue, they had no idea that three doors away, at 397 Massachusetts Avenue, was the house in which Martin Luther King Jr. was living while a graduate student at Boston University."

56. Cone, *Martin & Malcolm & America*, 207.

57. Gallen, *Malcolm X As They Knew Him*, 84.

58. Baldwin, "Of Their Spiritual Strivings," 124; Howard-Pitney, *Martin Luther King Jr., Malcolm X, and the Civil Rights Struggle*, 15–16.

59. Malcolm X, *February 1965*, 143, 150.

60. Malcolm X, *Malcolm X Talks to Young People*, 25-26.

61. Malcolm X, *Autobiography of Malcolm X*, 292.

62. Ibid.

63. Ibid., 383; Malcolm X, *February 1965*, 231.

64. Malcolm X, interviewed by Claude Lewis, December 1964, quoted in Goldman, *Death and Life of Malcolm X*, 222.

65. Clarke, *Malcolm X*, 91.

66. Goldman, *Death and Life of Malcolm X*, 4.

67. Strickland, *Malcolm X*, 230.

68. Malcolm X, *Autobiography of Malcolm X*, 385, 389.

6 An Identity Rooted in Humanity

1. Langley, "Malcolm X Promises U.S," 1.

2. Malcolm X, *February 1965*, 62.

3. Gardner, *Leading Minds*, 283.

4. Tinker, *Spirit and Resistance*, 104.

5. Suu Kyi and Clements, *Voice of Hope*, 193.

6. Thurman, *Luminous Darkness*, 94.

7. Thurman, "The Commitment," a sermon preached at The Church for the Fellowship of All Peoples, San Francisco, Calif., quoted in Pollard, *Mysticism and Social Change*, 73.

8. Thurman, *Luminous Darkness*, 98.

9. Malcolm X, *Malcolm X Speaks*, 116.

10. Thurman, *Luminous Darkness*, 99.

11. Malcolm X, "Whatever Is Necessary," 186.

12. Malcolm X, *February 1965*, 84.

13. Freire, *Pedagogy of the Oppressed*, 28. I find Freire helpful in understanding the dynamics of dehumanization in society. Yet, even using the terms "oppressor" and "oppressed" strip individuals and peoples of their personhood. Writing from a Native American perspective, George Tinker provides a helpful caution for this endeavor:

American Indian peoples resist categorization in terms of class structure. Instead, we insist on being recognized as "peoples," even nations with a claim to national sovereignty based on ancient title to our land. Whether we are categorized as "working class" or "the poor," such classification exacerbates the erosion of each distinct Native group's cultural integrity and national agenda. As much as capitalist economic structures—including the church (missionaries) and the academy (e.g., anthropologists)—have reduced American Indian peoples to nonpersonhood, so too the marxist model also fails to recognize our distinct personhood. Reducing our identity as discrete nations to that of a generic feckless socioeconomic class imposes upon us a particular culture of poverty and an especially disruptive culture of labor. It begs the question as to whether indigenous peoples desire production in the modern economic sense in the first place. To put the means of production into the hands of the poor inevitably induces the poor to be exploiters of indigenous peoples and their natural resources. Finally, it runs the serious risk of violating the very spiritual values that hold an indigenous cultural group together as a people. This criticism is not intended to suggest a blanket rejection of any tools of analysis, marxist or otherwise; rather, it is intended as a constructive critique of the normative models, and of the implicit hegemony they exercise in much of our midst in the Third World (*Spirit and Resistance*, 102-103).

14. Paris, *Black Religious Leaders*, 258.

15. Fanon, *Black Skin, White Masks*, 93.

16. Malcolm X, *Autobiography of Malcolm X*, 56–57.

17. Malcolm X, *Malcolm X on Afro-American History*, 25.

18. Malcolm X, *Speeches at Harvard*, 165.

19. Malcolm X, *February 1965*, 156–157.

20. Fanon, *Black Skin, White Masks*, 98.

21. Césaire, *Discourse on Colonialism*, 41.

22. Freire, *Pedagogy of the Oppressed*, 30. See Clasby, "Malcolm X and Liberation Theology," 176.

23. West, *Race Matters*, 96.

24. Malcolm X, *End of White World Supremacy*, 25.

25. Franklin, *Liberating Visions*, 92.

26. Bianchi, *Religious Experience of Revolutionaries*, 91.

27. Ibid.

28. Malcolm X, *Autobiography of Malcolm X*, 199. See Clasby, "Malcolm X and Liberation Theology," 179.

29. Sales, *From Civil Rights to Black Liberation*, 87.

30. T'Shaka, *Political Legacy of Malcolm X*, 90.

31. West, *Race Matters*, 99–100.

32. LaDuke, "Rebuilding Community," 56.

33. Freire, *Pedagogy of the Oppressed*, 43.

34. Ibid., 46–47.

35. Bonhoeffer, *Discipleship*, 285.

36. Kelly and Nelson, *Cost of Moral Leadership*, 144.

37. Suu Kyi, *Freedom from Fear*, 174.

38. Ibid.

39. Keane, "Introduction," viii-ix.

40. Suu Kyi and Clements, *Voice of Hope*, 135.

41. Ibid., 178.

42. Mandela, *Long Walk to Freedom*, 751. See also Daloz, et al., *Common Fire*, 77–79.

7 Aung San Suu Kyi: "A Revolution of the Spirit"

1. Victor, *Lady*, 27.

2. Suu Kyi, *Freedom from Fear*, 183.

3. Victor, *Lady*, 72.

4. Ibid., 78.

5. Ibid., 52.

6. Ibid.

7. Aris, "Introduction," xvii.

8. Victor, *Lady*, 83.

9. Suu Kyi, *Letters from Burma*, 120.

10. Parenteau, *Prisoner for Peace*, 92.

11. Suu Kyi, *Letters from Burma*, 119.

12. Ibid., 120.

13. Hunt, *Future of Peace*, 17.

14. Victor, *Lady*, 84.

15. Suu Kyi, *Freedom from Fear,* 193.

16. Ibid.

17. Ibid. See also Hunt, *Future of Peace*, 18.

18. Kreager, "Aung San Suu Kyi and the Peaceful Struggle for Human Rights in Burma," 326.

19. Ibid., 333.

20. Ibid., 327.

21. Parenteau, *Prisoner for Peace*, 106.

22. Suu Kyi, *Letters from Burma*, 121.

23. Than E, "A Flowering of the Spirit," 290.

24. Victor, *Lady*, 90.

25. Kreager, "Aung San Suu Kyi and the Peaceful Struggle for Human Rights in Burma," 336.

26. Ibid., 340.

27. Hunt, *Future of Peace*, 38.

28. Amnesty International, *Myanmar (Burma): Prisoners of Conscience*, 59.

29. Suu Kyi and Clements, *Voice of Hope*, 130.

30. Victor, *Lady*, 116.

31. Aris, "Introduction," xxii-xxiii.

32. Kreager, "Aung San Suu Kyi and the Peaceful Struggle for Human Rights in Burma," 319, 322.

33. Ibid., 321.

34. Victor, *Lady*, 107, 108.

35. Ibid., 39.

36. Ibid., 142.

37. Ibid., 130–131.

38. Ibid., 135.

39. Suu Kyi, *Freedom from Fear*, 360–361.

40. Victor, *Lady*, 139–140.

8 The Ethics of Revolution

1. Suu Kyi and Clements, *Voice of Hope*, 75–76.

2. Malcolm X, *The Autobiography of Malcolm X*, 376.

3. King, "From Beyond Vietnam," 145.

4. Hick, "Gandhi," 150.

5. T'Shaka, *Political Legacy of Malcolm X*, 209.

6. Dietrich Bonhoeffer, *Gesammelte Schriften*, 6 vols. (Munich: Christian Kaiser Verlag, 1958-1974), 4:86, quoted and translated by Thomas Day, *Dietrich Bonhoeffer on Christian Community and Common Sense* (Toronto: Edwin Mellen, 1982), 82.

7. Baldwin, "Malcolm and Martin," 269.

8. Lincoln, *Religion, Rebellion, Revolution*, 8.

9. Malcolm X, *Two Speeches by Malcolm X*, 25.

10. Gutiérrez, *Theology of Liberation*, 48.

11. Dyson, *I May Not Get There With You*, 39.

12. When a revolution of the spirit is dismissed, blocked, or sabotaged by the status quo, other visions of revolutionary activity emerge. Malcolm X declared of the world situation in the 1960s: "Time is on the side of the oppressed today. It's against the oppressor. Truth is on the side of the oppressed today, it's against the oppressor. You don't need anything else. I would just like to say this in my conclusion. You'll see terrorism that will terrify you, and if you don't think you'll see it, you're trying to blind yourself to the historic development of everything that's taking place on this earth today" (Malcolm X, *Two Speeches by Malcolm X*, 25). Perhaps the increased terrorism of the early years of the twenty-first century is a result of ignoring calls by mystic-activists in the twentieth century for a revolution of the spirit. Malcolm X's comments forty years earlier seem to have foretold this. Is it possible that since a revolution of the spirit was embraced by so few, a revolution of terror emerged? Is it possible that in the absence of social justice in the world, a new horrific form of protest has emerged on the world stage?

13. Goldman, *Death and Life of Malcolm X*, 398-399.

14. Bonhoeffer, *Ethics*, 188.

15. Levinas, *Difficult Freedom*, 17. See also Soelle, *The Silent Cry*, 199.

16. DeCaro, *On the Side of My People*, 2.

17. Brady, *Moral Bond of Community*, 84.

18. Ibid., 84–85.

19. Sanders, *Empowerment Ethics for a Liberated People*, 1.

20. Ibid., 2.

21. Ibid., 7.

22. Brady, *Moral Bond of Community*, 42.

23. Ibid.

24. Ibid.

25. Wiesel, *Town Beyond the Wall*, 149.

26. Menchú, *I, Rigoberta Menchú*, 245–246.

27. Brady, *Moral Bond of Community*, 44.

28. Menchú, *I, Rigoberta Menchú*, 118.

29. King, *I Have a Dream*, 5.

30. Brady, *Moral Bond of Community*, 42.

31. Brueggemann, *Prophetic Imagination*, 65.

32. King, *I Have a Dream*, 104–105.

33. Lischer, *Preacher King*, 177.

34. E. U. Essien-Udom, *Black Nationalism*, 101.

35. The focus of this book is not gender roles and social justice activists. Yet a few observations are in order. One issue directly related to gender and leadership in social movements is how the family roles are divided. Women often delay their entrance into activism because of raising children. Rigoberta Menchú became an activist at an early age because she chose not to marry and have children until after the struggle. On the other hand, men often selfishly disregard marriage and family. Martin Luther King Jr. expected his wife to stay home and raise the children. Coretta Scott King wanted to play a more public role in the movement but her husband blocked her. Male leaders often spend long hours in activism.

The generation of leaders emerging in the twenty-first century needs to critique their twentieth-century predecessors in terms of how gender roles intersect with leadership. The twentieth century was a man's world. Most leaders of social movements were men. When women did lead, it was often an exception to the rule and usually their work needed validation from males.

I notice an interesting progression in gender status (and class status) of the twentieth-century leaders examined in this book, which portends well for the future. In the early part of the twentieth century, Dietrich Bonhoeffer represents leadership against injustice from an educated and privileged class. Mohandas Gandhi, while oppressed under British rule, also represents an educated portion of society and was a part of the dominant class in India. In the middle of the century, Martin Luther King Jr. represents a status similar to Gandhi except that he was a member of a minority group. Alongside King, though, was Malcolm X who was from a grassroots oppressed group and self-educated. Also, women like Dorothy Day renounced white privilege to live and work among the poor, and Fannie Lou Hamer emerged from the grassroots as a regional leader with some national exposure.

By the last part of the twentieth century, men similar to Bonhoeffer, Gandhi, King, and Malcolm X (for example Nelson Mandela and Lech Walesa) and women similar to Day and Hamer were still in leadership. Yet women leading major freedom movements emerge, such as Aung San Suu Kyi and Rigoberta Menchú—both of whom were recognized with the Nobel Peace Prize. In the case of Suu Kyi and Menchú, both have fathers whose legacy they inherit (and surpass). Whether they would have risen to such heights in leadership without the validation of their fathers' mantle of leadership is open to debate. In the case of Suu Kyi, the aura of her father surrounded and empowered her own entrance into leadership in the Burmese struggle for independence. This in no way diminishes her leadership. It does raise the question of the ways sexism affects who leads in society.

I observe a possibility for progress, though, in the shift from elite and educated men in mystic-activist leadership in the first third of the twentieth century, to a middle third that also includes men from the grassroots and the poor, as well as some women in regional leadership, to the final third where women emerge as major leaders—albeit still needing the validation of men in a sexist society.

The twenty-first century holds the potential for more women in leadership on their own terms. This means that men must take more responsibility and interest in an egalitarian partnership in their marriages and greater involvement in the lives of the children. Social justice and reconciliation are not merely the concerns of politics. They should begin in the home. Creative ways of leading may need to be embraced. Team leadership may become more evident.

36. Carmichael, *Ready for Revolution*, 711–712.
37. Stoll, *Rigoberta Menchú and the Story of All Poor Guatemalans*.
38. Menchú, *I, Rigoberta Menchú*, 1.
39. Suu Kyi, *Freedom from Fear*, 225.
40. Kelly, "Prayer and Action for Justice," 252.
41. Césaire, *Discourse on Colonialism*, 31.
42. Pollard, *Mysticism and Social Change*, 91.
43. Suu Kyi and Clements, *Voice of Hope*, 19.
44. Thomas Merton, *Seeds of Destruction*, 42.
46. Falk, *Religion and Humane Global Governance*, 105.

47. Boesak, *Tenderness of Conscience*, 201.
48. Ibid., 207.
49. Bonhoeffer, *Ethics*, 118–119.
50. Suu Kyi, *Freedom from Fear*, 183.

9 A Lived Faith

1. Marsh, *God's Long Summer*, 12.
2. Ibid., 19.
3. Ibid., 20.
4. "Fannie Lou Hamer, conversation with SNCC worker Dale Grunemeier, Ruleville, Mississippi, 1964," quoted in Marsh, *God's Long Summer*, 22.
5. Ibid.
6. Charles McLaurin, "Voice of Calm," 12.
7. Fannie Lou Hamer in *Freedom on My Mind*, documentary film produced and directed by Connie Field and Marilyn Mulford (Berkeley: Clarity Educational, 1994), quoted in Marsh, *God's Long Summer*, 25.
8. Soelle, *Silent Cry*, 3.
9. Brown, *Gandhi*, 123.
10. Heschel, *Moral Grandeur*, vii-viii.
11. Ibid., 185.
12. King, *I Have a Dream*, 58.
13. Kelly and Nelson, *Cost of Moral Leadership*, 41. I prefer this translation to the one found in Bonhoeffer, *Letters and Papers from Prison*, 300.
14. Malcolm X, *Speeches at Harvard*, 164.
15. Malcolm X, interviewed by Milton Henry, 25 July 1964, Cairo, for broadcast on *The GOAL Show* (Detroit: WGPR), quoted in DeCaro, *On the Side of My People*, 237.
16. Malcolm X, *Malcolm X Speaks*, 60.
17. Suu Kyi and Clements, *Voice of Hope*, 165.
18. Ibid., 166.
19. Ibid., 39.
20. Wiesel, "The Urgency of Hope," 48.
21. Ibid., 59.
22. Thurman, *Strange Freedom*, 110.
23. King, *I Have a Dream*, 61.
24. Suu Kyi and Clements, *Voice of Hope*, 174.
25. Bonhoeffer, *Letters & Papers from Prison*, 3.
26. Ibid., 5.
27. Nasr, "What Attracted Merton to Sufism," 9
28. Thurman, *Strange Freedom*, 109.
29. Gandhi, *Vows and Observances*, 144.
30. Fasching and Dechant, *Comparative Religious Ethics*, 7, 48, 68–70.
31. Ibid., 6.
32. Ibid., 156.
33. Holmes, *Joy Unspeakable*, 155, 156, 157.
34. Inchausti, *Subversive Orthodoxy*, 106
35. Hunt, *Future of Peace*, 35.
36. Nhat Hanh, *Living Buddha, Living Christ*, 136.
37. Vincent Harding writes: "To see King as he was in those last weeks of his life,

even at the simplest levels of our perception, is to see an exhausted, hard pressed, at times beleaguered-looking brother (didn't Malcolm look that way in his last days?), far older than the thirty-nine years of his life, often saying, 'I'm tired now, I've been in this thing thirteen years and now I'm really tired.' ... To look carefully into King's last weeks, then is to see darkness, both the creative and the perilous darkness of the wilderness" (Harding, *Martin Luther King*, 86).

38. Deats, *Martin Luther King, Jr.*, 129, 130.

39. Soelle, *Silent Cry*, 252.

Epilogue: Reconciliation and Religion in the Twenty-First Century

1. Gopin, *Holy War, Holy Peace*, 45. See 40–57 for a full description of this process and to read a draft of the covenant. I am indebted to Marc Gopin's book for generating many of the ideas I present in this epilogue.

2. Ibid, 47. For a more recent comment by Gopin on the need for engaging the religious aspect of peacemaking in the Holy Land, see Marc Gopin, "Israel's Lost Opportunity: A Failure to Communicate," *Christian Century*, May 30, 2006, 8–9.

3. Ibid, 45.

4. Lischer, *End of Words*, 164.

5. Boesak, *Tenderness of Conscience*, 182.

6. Ibid., 185.

7. Ibid., 186.

8. Ibid., 185–186.

9. Gopin, *Holy War, Holy Peace*, 152.

10. Ibid., 154.

11. Ibid., 153.

12. Ibid., 44. Eliyahu McLean is mentioned by Gopin and also in Halevi, *At the Entrance to the Garden of Eden*, as a central figure in this effort of building relationships. He and others have formed an interfaith reconciliation network called Jerusalem Peacemakers. They are indeed mystic-activists in the Holy Land. For more information go to: www.jerusalempeacemakers.org.

13. Abu-Nimer, *Reconciliation, Justice, and Coexistence*, 182.

14. D'Souza, "Creating Spaces," 186.

15. See Halevi, *At the Entrance to the Garden of Eden*. Yossi Halevi is an Israeli journalist and observant Jew who wanted to build relationships with Muslims and Christians in the Holy Land. He did not want to do this just through conversation. He wanted to join them in the places and times of worship. Eliyahu McLean served as a guide on this journey, which occurred during the same time period that the religious peace covenant was developing. Reading Halevi's book provides a wonderful glimpse into the worship practices of persons involved in interfaith reconciliation efforts in the late 1990s. Interfaith reconciliation efforts with worship as a primary component have continued in the Holy Land since 2001 through the Sulha Peace Project (www.sulha.com).

16. Abu-Nimer, "The Miracles of Transformation through Interfaith Dialogue," 18.

17. Nhat Hanh, *Living Buddha, Living Christ*, 99–100. He states that he has images of both Buddha and Christ on his altar.

18. Gopin, *Holy War, Holy Peace*, 155.

19. Ibid.

20. Ibid., 27.

BIBLIOGRAPHY

Abu-Nimer, Mohammed. *Reconciliation, Justice, and Coexistence: Theory and Practice.* New York: Lexington, 2001.

———. "The Miracles of Transformation through Interfaith Dialogue: Are You a Believer?" In *Interfaith Dialogue and Peacebuilding,* edited by David R. Smock, 15-32. Washington, D.C.: United States Institute of Peace, 2002.

Al-Hadid, Amiri YaSin. "Al-Qur'an and Sunnah: From Malcolm X to El-Hajj Malik El-Shabazz." In *Between the Cross and the Crescent: Christian and Muslim Perspectives on Malcolm and Martin,* edited by Lewis V. Baldwin and Amiri YaSin Al-Hadid, 49-82. Gainesville: University Press of Florida, 2002.

Amnesty International. *Myanmar (Burma): Prisoners of Conscience. A Chronicle of Developments since September 1988* (November 1989).

Aris, Michael. "Introduction." In *Freedom from Fear,* rev. ed., by Aung San Suu Kyi, xvii-xxxi. London: Penguin, 1995.

Aung San Suu Kyi. *Freedom from Fear and Other Writings.* Rev. ed. London: Penguin, 1995.

———. *Letters from Burma.* London: Penguin, 1997.

———, and Alan Clements. *The Voice of Hope.* New York: Seven Stories, 1997.

Baker, Rob, and Gray Henry, eds. *Merton & Sufism: The Untold Story.* Louisville: Fons Vitae, 1999.

Baldwin, James. "Malcolm and Martin." In *Malcolm X: As They Knew Him,* edited by David Gallen, 257-279. New York: Carroll & Graf, 1992.

Baldwin, Lewis V., and Amiri YaSin Al-Hadid. *Between the Cross and the Crescent: Christian and Muslim Perspectives on Malcolm and Martin.* Gainesville: University Press of Florida, 2002.

Baldwin, Lewis V. "Of Their Spiritual Strivings: Malcolm and Martin on Religion and Freedom." In *Between the Cross and the Crescent: Christian and Muslim Perspectives on Malcolm and Martin,* Lewis V. Baldwin and Amiri YaSin Al-Hadid, 83-127. Gainesville: University Press of Florida, 2002.

Baranowski, Shelley. "The Confessing Church and Anti-Semitism: Protestant Identity, German Nationhood, and the Exclusion of the Jews." In *Betrayal: German Churches and the Holocaust,* edited by Robert P. Ericksen and Susannah Heschel, 90-109. Minneapolis: Fortress Press, 1999.

Barnes, Kenneth C. "Dietrich Bonhoeffer and Hitler's Persecution of the Jews." In *Betrayal: German Churches and the Holocaust,* edited by Robert P. Ericksen and Susannah Heschel,110-128. Minneapolis: Fortress Press, 1999.

Baum, Gregory. *The Church for Others: Protestant Theology in Communist East Germany.* Grand Rapids: Eerdmans, 1996.

Bergen, Doris L. "Storm Troopers of Christ: The German Christian Movement and the Ecclesiastical Final Solution." In *Betrayal: German Churches and the Holocaust,* edited by Robert P. Ericksen and Susannah Heschel, 40-67. Minneapolis: Fortress Press, 1999.

Bethge, Eberhard. "Dietrich Bonhoeffer and the Jews." In *Ethical Responsibility: Bonhoeffer's Legacy to the Churches*, edited by John D. Godsey and Geffrey B. Kelly, 43-96. New York: Edwin Mellen, 1981.

———. *Dietrich Bonhoeffer: Man of Vision, Man of Courage*. Rev. ed. Minneapolis: Fortress Press, 2000.

Bianchi, Eugene C. *The Religious Experience of Revolutionaries*. Garden City: Doubleday, 1972.

Boesak, Allan A. "What Dietrich Bonhoeffer Has Meant to Me." In *Bonhoeffer's Ethics: Old Europe and New Frontiers*, edited by Guy Carter, René van Eyden, Hans-Dirk van Hoogstraten, and Jurgen Wiersma, 21-29. Kampen: Kok Pharos, 1991.

———. *The Tenderness of Conscience: African Renaissance and the Spirituality of Politics*. Stellenbosch: SUN, 2005.

Bonhoeffer, Dietrich. *Discipleship*. Vol. 4, Dietrich Bonhoeffer Works. Edited by John D. Godsey and Geffrey B. Kelly. Minneapolis: Fortress Press, 2000.

———. *Ethics*. New York: Macmillan Publishing, 1965.

———. *Gesammelte Schriften*. Vol. I. Ed. Eberhard Bethge. Munich: Chr. Kaiser, 1965.

———. *Letters and Papers from Prison*. Enl. Ed. New York, Macmillan, 1972.

———. *Life Together/Prayerbook of the Bible*. Vol. 5, Dietrich Bonhoeffer Works. Edited by James H. Burtness and Geffrey B. Kelly. Minneapolis: Fortress Press, 1996.

———. *No Rusty Swords: Letters, Lectures and Notes, 1928-1936*. Vol. I, Collected Works of Dietrich Bonhoeffer, edited by Edwin Robertson. New York: Harper & Row, 1965.

———. *A Testament to Freedom: The Essential Writings of Dietrich Bonhoeffer*. Edited by Geffrey B. Kelly and F. Burton Nelson. San Francisco: HarperCollins, 1990.

———. *The Way to Freedom: Letters, Lectures and Notes, 1935-1939*. Vol. II, Collected Works of Dietrich Bonhoeffer, edited by Edwin Robertson. London: Collins, 1966.

Brady, Bernard V. *The Moral Bond of Community: Justice and Discourse in Christian Morality*. Washington, D.C.: Georgetown University Press, 1998.

Brown, Judith M. *Gandhi: Prisoner of Hope*. New Haven: Yale University Press, 1989.

Brueggemann, Walter. *The Prophetic Imagination*. 2nd ed. Minneapolis: Fortress Press, 2001.

Burgos-Debray, Elisabeth. "Introduction." In *I, Rigoberta Menchú: An Indian Women in Guatemala*, by Rigoberta Menchú, xi-xxi. London: Verso, 1984.

Carmichael, Stokely, with Ekwueme Michael Thelwell. *Ready for Revolution: The Life and Struggles of Stokely Carmichael (Kwame Ture)*. New York: Scribner, 2003.

Carmody, Denise Lardner, and John Tully Carmody. *Mysticism: Holiness East and West*. New York: Oxford University Press, 1996.

———. *Peace and Justice in the Scriptures of the World Religions*. Mahwah: Paulist, 1988.

Carter, Guy, René van Eyden, Hans-Dirk van Hoogstraten, and Jurgen Wiersma, eds. *Bonhoeffer's Ethics: Old Europe and New Frontiers*. Kampen: Kok Pharos, 1991.

Césaire, Aimé. *Discourse on Colonialism.* Rev. ed. New York: Monthly Review, 2000.

Clarke, John. H., ed. *Malcolm X: The Man and His Times.* Trenton: African World, 1990.

Clasby, Nancy Tenfelde. "Malcolm X and Liberation Theology." *Cross Currents* (Summer 1988).

Clingan, Ralph Garlin. *Against Cheap Grace in a World Come of Age: An Intellectual Biography of Clayton Powell, 1865-1953.* New York: Peter Lang, 2002.

Collins, Rodnell P. *Seventh Child: A Family Memoir of Malcolm X.* With Peter A. Bailey. Secaucus: Birch Lane, 1998.

Cohen, Abraham. *Everyman's Talmud.* New York: Schocken, 1975

Cone, James H. *Black Theology & Black Power.* New York: Seabury, 1969.

——. *Martin & Malcolm & America: A Dream or a Nightmare.* Maryknoll: Orbis, 1991.

Coward, Harold, and Gordon S. Smith, eds. *Religion and Peacebuilding.* Albany: SUNY Press, 2004.

Dalai Lama. *Ethics for the New Millennium.* New York: Riverhead, 1999.

Daloz, Laurent A. Parks, Cheryl H. Keen, James P. Keen, and Sharon Daloz Parks. *Common Fire: Lives of Commitment in a Complex World.* Boston: Beacon, 1996.

Day, Dorothy. *The Long Loneliness.* New York: Harper & Row, 1952.

Deats, Richard. *Martin Luther King, Jr.: Spirit-Led Prophet.* Rev. ed. Hyde Park: New City, 2003.

DeCaro, Louis A., Jr. *Malcolm and the Cross.* New York: New York University Press, 1998.

——. *On the Side of My People: A Religious Life of Malcolm X.* New York: New York University Press, 1996.

De Gruchy, John W. *Bonhoeffer and South Africa: Theology in Dialogue.* Grand Rapids: Eerdmans, 1984.

——., ed. *The Cambridge Companion to Dietrich Bonhoeffer.* Cambridge, Mass.: Cambridge University Press, 1999.

Dennis, Marie, Renny Golden, and Scott Wright. *Oscar Romero: Reflections on His Life and Writings.* Maryknoll: Orbis, 2000.

DeYoung, Curtiss Paul. *Coming Together: The Bible's Message in an Age of Diversity.* Valley Forge: Judson, 1995.

——. *Reconciliation: Our Greatest Challenge, Our Only Hope.* Valley Forge: Judson, 1997.

D'Souza, Diane. "Creating Spaces: Interreligious Initiatives for Peace." In *Religion and Peacebuilding,* edited by, Harold Coward and Gordon S. Smith, 169-189. Albany: SUNY Press, 2004.

Dyson, Michael Eric. *I May Not Get There With You: The True Martin Luther King, Jr.* New York: Free, 2000.

Ericksen, Robert P., and Susannah Heschel, eds. *Betrayal: German Churches and the Holocaust.* Minneapolis: Fortress Press, 1999.

Erickson, Robert P., and Susannah Heschel, "Introduction." In *Betrayal: German Churches and the Holocaust,* Robert P. Ericksen and Susannah Heschel, eds., 1-21. Minneapolis: Fortress Press, 1999.

Essien-Udom, E. U. *Black Nationalism: The Search for an Identity in America.* Chicago: University of Chicago Press, 1963.

Evanzz, Karl. *The Judas Factor: The Plot to Kill Malcolm X.* New York: Thunder Mouth's, 1992.

———. *The Messenger: The Rise and Fall of Elijah Muhammad.* New York: Pantheon, 1999.

Falk, Richard. *Religion and Humane Global Governance.* New York: Palgrave, 2001.

Fanon, Frantz. *Black Skin, White Masks.* New York: Grove, 1967.

Fasching, Darrell J., and Dell Dechant. *Comparative Religious Ethics: A Narrative Approach.* Oxford: Blackwell, 2001.

Floyd, Wayne Whitson, Jr., and Charles Marsh, eds. *Theology and the Practice of Responsibility: Essays on Dietrich Bonhoeffer.* Valley Forge: Trinity, 1994.

Franklin, Robert. *Liberating Visions: Human Fulfillment and Social Justice in African-American Thought.* Minneapolis: Fortress Press, 1990.

Freire, Paulo. *Pedagogy of the Oppressed.* New York: Seabury, 1970.

Galilea, Segundo. "Liberation as an Encounter with Politics and Contemplation." In *The Mystical and Political Dimension of the Christian Faith,* edited by Claude Geffré and Gustavo Gutiérrez, 19-33. New York: Herder and Herder, 1974.

Gallen, David, ed. *Malcolm X: As They Knew Him.* New York: Carroll & Graf, 1992.

Gandhi, Mohandas K. *Vows and Observances.* Berkeley.: Berkeley Hills, 1999.

Gardner, Howard. *Creating Minds: An Anatomy of Creativity Seen Through the Lives of Freud, Einstein, Picasso, Stravinsky, Eliot, Graham and Gandhi.* New York: Basic, 1993.

———. *Leading Minds: An Anatomy of Leadership.* New York: Basic, 1995.

Garrow, David. *Bearing the Cross: Martin Luther King, Jr. and Southern Christian Leadership Conference.* New York: William Morrow, 1986.

Geffré, Claude, and Gustavo Gutiérrez, eds. *The Mystical and Political Dimension of the Christian Faith.* New York: Herder and Herder, 1974.

Godsey, John D., and Geffrey B. Kelly, eds. *Ethical Responsibility: Bonhoeffer's Legacy to the Churches.* New York: Edwin Mellen, 1981.

Goldman, Peter. *The Death and Life of Malcolm X.* 2nd ed. Urbana: University of Illinois Press, 1979.

Gopin, Marc. *Holy War, Holy Peace: How Religion Can Bring Peace to the Middle East.* New York: Oxford University Press, 2002.

Gottlieb, Roger S. *Joining Hands: Politics and Religion Together for Social Change.* Cambridge, Mass.: Westview, 2002.

Gutiérrez, Gustavo. *The Power of the Poor in History.* Maryknoll: Orbis, 1983.

———. *A Theology of Liberation.* Maryknoll: Orbis, 1973.

Halevi, Yossi Klein. *At the Entrance to the Garden of Eden: A Jew's Search for Hope with Christians and Muslims in the Holy Land.* San Francisco: Perennial, 2002.

Harding, Vincent. *Martin Luther King: The Inconvenient Hero.* Maryknoll: Orbis, 1996.

Heschel, Abraham Joshua. *Moral Grandeur and Spiritual Audacity: Essays [of] Abraham Joshua Heschel.* Ed. Susannah Heschel. New York: Farrar, Straus, & Giroux, 1996.

Heschel, Susannah. "When Jesus Was an Aryan: The Protestant Church and Anti-Semitic Propaganda." In *Betrayal: German Churches and the Holocaust,* edited by Robert P. Ericksen and Susannah Heschel, 68-89. Minneapolis: Fortress Press, 1999.

Hick, John. "Gandhi: The Fusion of Religion and Politics." In *Religion, Politics, and Peace*, edited by LeRoy S. Rouner, 145-164. Notre Dame, Ind.: University of Notre Dame Press, 1999.

Holmes, Barbara A. *Joy Unspeakable: Contemplative Practices of the Black Church*. Minneapolis: Fortress Press, 2004.

Holt, Bradley P. *Thirsty for God: A Brief History of Christian Spirituality*. Minneapolis: Fortress Press, 2005.

Howard-Pitney, David. *Martin Luther King Jr., Malcolm X, and the Civil Rights Struggle of the 1950s and 1960s: A Brief History with Documents*. Boston: Bedford/St. Martin's, 2004.

Hunt, Scott A. *The Future of Peace: On the Front Lines with the World's Greatest Peacemakers*. San Francisco: HarperSanFrancisco, 2002.

Inchausti, Robert. *Subversive Orthodoxy: Outlaws, Revolutionaries, and other Christians in Disguise*. Grand Rapids: Brazos, 2005.

Jordens, J. T. F. *Gandhi's Religion: A Homespun Shawl*. New York: St. Martin's, 1998.

Karim, Benjamin. "Introduction." In *The End of White World Supremacy: Four Speeches by Malcolm X*, edited by Benjamin Karim. New York: Arcade, 1971.

———. *Remembering Malcolm*. With Peter Skutches and David Gallen. New York: Carroll & Graf, 1992.

Keane, Fergal. "Introduction." In *Letters from Burma*, by Aung San Suu Kyi, vii-xi. London: Penguin, 1997.

Kelly, Geffrey B. *Liberating Faith: Bonhoeffer's Message for Today*. Minneapolis: Augsburg Publishing House, 1984.

———. "Bonhoeffer and Romero: Prophets of Justice for the Oppressed." In *Theology and the Practice of Responsibility: Essays on Dietrich Bonhoeffer*, edited by Wayne Whitson Floyd Jr. and Charles Marsh, 85-105. Valley Forge: Trinity, 1994.

———. "Prayer and Action for Justice: Bonhoeffer's Spirituality." In *The Cambridge Companion to Dietrich Bonhoeffer*, edited by John W. de Gruchy, 246-268. Cambridge, Mass.: Cambridge University Press, 1999.

Kelly, Geffrey B., and F. Burton Nelson. "Solidarity with the Oppressed: Bonhoeffer the Man." In *A Testament to Freedom: The Essential Writings of Dietrich Bonhoeffer*, Dietrich Bonhoeffer (eds. Geffrey B. Kelly and F. Burton Nelson), 1-46. San Francisco: HarperCollins, 1990.

Kelly, Geffrey B., and F. Burton Nelson, eds. *The Cost of Moral Leadership: The Spirituality of Dietrich Bonhoeffer*. Grand Rapids: Eerdmans, 2003.

———. *A Testament to Freedom: The Essential Writings of Dietrich Bonhoeffer*. San Francisco: HarperCollins, 1990.

King: A Filmed Record…Montgomery to Memphis. Produced and directed by Sidney Lumet and Joseph L. Mankiewicz. 1970. Documentary film.

King, Martin Luther, Jr. "From Beyond Vietnam." In *Martin Luther King Jr., Malcolm X, and the Civil Rights Struggle of the 1950s and 1960s: A Brief History with Documents*, by David Howard-Pitney, 138-147. Boston: Bedford/St. Martin's, 2004.

———. *I Have a Dream: Writings and Speeches that Changed the World*. Edited by James M. Washington. San Francisco: HarperCollins, 1992.

———. *Stride Toward Freedom: The Montgomery Story*. New York: Harper & Brothers, 1958.

Kreager, Philip. "Aung San Suu Kyi and the Peaceful Struggle for Human Rights in Burma." In *Freedom from Fear*, rev. ed., by Aung San Suu Kyi, 318-359. London: Penguin, 1995.

LaDuke, Winona. "Rebuilding Community." Interview by Penny Rosenwasser. In *Visionary Voices: Women on Power*, edited by Penny Rosenwasser, 55-68. San Francisco: Aunt Lute, 1992.

Langley, Christopher. "Malcolm X Promises U.S. a Long, Bloody Summer," *The Dartmouth*. Dartmouth College, Hanover (27 January 1965).

Lawrence-Lightfoot, Sara, and Jessica Hoffman Davis. *The Art and Science of Portraiture*. San Francisco: Jossey-Bass, 1997.

Lawrence-Lightfoot, Sara. "Introduction: The Frame." In *The Art and Science of Portraiture*, Sara Lawrence-Lightfoot and Jessica Hoffman Davis, xv-xvii. San Francisco: Jossey-Bass, 1997.

_____. "A View of the Whole: Origins and Purposes." In *The Art and Science of Portraiture*, Sara Lawrence-Lightfoot and Jessica Hoffman Davis, 1-16. San Francisco: Jossey-Bass, 1997.

_____. "Illumination: Expressing a Point of View." In *The Art and Science of Portraiture*, Sara Lawrence-Lightfoot and Jessica Hoffman Davis, 83-105. San Francisco: Jossey-Bass, 1997.

_____. "Illumination: Navigating Intimacy." In *The Art and Science of Portraiture*, Sara Lawrence-Lightfoot and Jessica Hoffman Davis, 133-159. San Francisco: Jossey-Bass, 1997.

Levinas, Emmanuel. *Difficult Freedom: Essays on Judaism*. Translated by Seán Hand. Baltimore: John Hopkins University Press, 1990.

Lincoln, Bruce, ed. *Religion, Rebellion, Revolution: An Interdisciplinary and Cross-cultural Collection of Essays*. New York: St. Martin's, 1985.

Lincoln, C. Eric. *The Black Muslims in America*. Rev. ed. Queens: Kayode, 1973.

Lischer, Richard. *The End of Words: The Language of Reconciliation in a Culture of Violence*. Grand Rapids: Eerdmans, 2005.

———. *The Preacher King: Martin Luther King, Jr. and the Word that Moved America*. New York: Oxford University Press, 1995.

Malcolm X. *The Autobiography of Malcolm X*. As told to Alex Haley. New York: Grove, 1965.

———. *By Any Means Necessary*. New York: Pathfinder, 1970.

———. *The End of White World Supremacy: Four Speeches by Malcolm X*. Edited by Benjamin Karim. New York: Arcade Publishing, 1971.

———. *February 1965: The Final Speeches*. New York: Pathfinder, 1992.

———. *Malcolm X on Afro-American History*. New York: Pathfinder, 1967.

———. *Malcolm X Speaks*. Ed. George Breitman. New York: Grove Weidenfeld, 1965.

———. *Malcolm X Speeches at Harvard*. Ed. Archie Epps. New York: Paragon House, 1991.

———. *Malcolm X Talks to Young People*. New York: Pathfinder, 1965.

———. *Two Speeches by Malcolm X*. 3rd. ed. New York: Pathfinder, 1990.

———. "Whatever Is Necessary: The Last Television Interview with Pierre Berton." In *Malcolm X: As They Knew Him*, edited by David Gallen, 177-187. New York: Carroll & Graf, 1992.

Mandela, Nelson. *Long Walk to Freedom*. London: Abacus, 1994.

Marsh, Charles. *God's Long Summer: Stories of Faith and Civil Rights*. Princeton: Princeton University Press, 1997.

McGinn, Bernard. *The Foundation of Mysticism: Origins to the Fifth Century*. New York: Crossroad, 1991.

McLaurin, Charles. "Voice of Calm." *Sojourners* 11:11 (December 1982).

Menchú, Rigoberta. *I, Rigoberta Menchú: An Indian Woman in Guatemala*. London: Verso, 1984.

Merton, Thomas. *Seeds of Destruction*. New York: Farrar, Straus & Company, 1964.

Murvar, Vatro. "Integrative and Revolutionary Capabilities of Religion." In *Religious Change and Continuity*, edited by Harry M. Johnson, 74-86. San Francisco: Jossey-Bass, 1979.

Nasr, Seyyed Hossein. "What Attracted Merton to Sufism." In *Merton & Sufism: The Untold Story*, edited by Rob Baker and Gray Henry, 9-13. Louisville: Fons Vitae, 1999.

Natambu, Kofi. *The Life and Work of Malcolm X*. Indianapolis: Alpha, 2002.

Nhat Hanh, Thich. *Living Buddha, Living Christ*. New York: Riverhead, 1995.

Noffke, Suzanne. "Introduction." In *Catherine of Siena: The Dialogue*, translated and introduction by Suzanne Noffke, 1-22. New York: Paulist, 1980.

Nouwen, Henri J. M. *Thomas Merton: Contemplative Critic*. Reprint (original title: *Pray to Live*). Notre Dame, Ind.: Fides, 1972; Liguori: Liguori/Triumph, 1991.

Parenteau, John. *Prisoner for Peace: Aung San Suu Kyi and Burma's Struggle for Democracy*. Greensboro: Morgan Reynolds, 1994.

Paris, Peter. *Black Religious Leaders: Conflict in Unity*. Louisville: Westminster/John Knox, 1991.

Perry, Bruce. *Malcolm: The Life of a Man Who Changed Black America*. Barrytown: Station Hill, 1991.

Plant, Stephen J. "Ethics and Materialist Hermeneutics." In *Theology and the Practice of Responsibility: Essays on Dietrich Bonhoeffer*, edited by Wayne Whitson Floyd, Jr. and Charles Marsh, 107-115. Valley Forge: Trinity, 1994.

Pollard, Alton B., III. *Mysticism and Social Change: The Social Witness of Howard Thurman*. New York: Peter Lang, 1992.

Robertson, Edwin. *The Shame and the Sacrifice: The Life and Martyrdom of Dietrich Bonhoeffer*. New York: Collier, 1988.

Romero, Oscar. *Voice of the Voiceless: The Four Pastoral Letters and Other Statements*. Translated by Michael J. Walsh. Maryknoll: Orbis, 1985.

Rosenwasser, Penny, ed. *Visionary Voices: Women on Power*. San Francisco: Aunt Lute, 1992.

Rouner, Leroy S., ed. *Religion, Politics, and Peace*. Notre Dame, Ind.: University of Notre Dame Press, 1999.

Sales, William. *From Civil Rights to Black Liberation: Malcolm X and the Organization of Afro-American Unity*. Boston: South End, 1994.

Sanders, Cheryl J. *Empowerment Ethics for a Liberated People: A Path to African American Social Transformation*. Minneapolis: Fortress Press, 1995.

Sidorenko, Konstantin. *Robert F. Kennedy: A Spiritual Biography*. New York: Crossroad, 2000.

Smock, David R., ed. *Interfaith Dialogue and Peacebuilding.* Washington, D.C.: United States Institute of Peace, 2002.

Soelle, Dorothee. *The Silent Cry: Mysticism and Resistance.* Minneapolis: Fortress Press, 2001.

Stoll, David. *Rigoberta Menchú and the Story of All Poor Guatemalans.* Boulder: Westview, 1999.

Strickland, William. *Malcolm X: Make it Plain.* Edited by Cheryll Y. Greene. New York: Viking, 1994.

Than E, Ma. "A Flowering of the Spirit: Memories of Suu and Her Family." In *Freedom from Fear,* rev. ed., by Aung San Suu Kyi, 275-291. London: Penguin, 1995.

Thurman, Howard. *The Luminous Darkness: A Personal Interpretation of the Anatomy of Segregation and the Ground of Hope.* New York: Harper & Row, 1965.

———. *Mysticism and the Experience of Love.* Wallingford: Pendle Hill, 1961.

———. *A Strange Freedom: The Best of Howard Thurman on Religious Experience and Public Life.* Edited by Walter Earl Fluker and Catherine Tumber. Boston: Beacon, 1998.

Tinker, George E. *Spirit and Resistance: Political Theology and American Indian Liberation.* Minneapolis: Fortress Press, 2004.

T'Shaka, Oba. *The Political Legacy of Malcolm X.* Richmond: Pan Afrikan, 1983.

Victor, Barbara. *The Lady: Aung San Suu Kyi, Nobel Laureate and Burma's Prisoner.* Rev. ed. Boston: Faber and Faber, 2002.

West, Cornel. "Malcolm X and Black Rage." In *Malcolm X in Our Own Image,* edited by Joe Wood, 48-58. New York: St. Martin's, 1992.

———. *Race Matters.* Boston: Beacon, 1993.

Wiersma, Jurgen. "Bonhoeffer and Gandhi: Measure and Movement for a Political Ethic of Resistance." In *Bonhoeffer's Ethics: Old Europe and New Frontiers,* edited by Guy Carter, René van Eyden, Hans-Dirk van Hoogstraten, and Jurgen Wiersma, 208-211. Kampen: Kok Pharos, 1991.

Wiesel, Elie. *The Town Beyond the Wall.* New York: Schocken, 1982.

———. "The Urgency of Hope." In *Religion, Politics, and Peace,* edited by Leroy S. Rouner, 48-60. Notre Dame, Ind.: University of Notre Dame Press, 1999.

Willie, Charles V. *Theories of Human Social Action.* Dix Hills: General Hall, 1994.

Witcover, Jules. *85 Days: The Last Campaign of Robert Kennedy.* New York: William Morrow, 1988.

Wolfenstein, Eugene V. *The Victims of Democracy: Malcolm X and the Black Revolution.* Berkeley: University of California Press, 1981.

Wood, Joe, ed. *Malcolm X in Our Own Image.* New York: St. Martin's, 1992.

Wüstenberg, Ralf K. *A Theology of Life: Dietrich Bonhoeffer's Religionless Christianity.* Grand Rapids: Eerdmans, 1988.

Young, Josiah Ulysses. *No Difference in the Fare: Dietrich Bonhoeffer and the Problem of Racism.* Grand Rapids: Eerdmans, 1998.

Zimmermann, Wolf-Dieter and Ronald Gregor, eds. *I Knew Dietrich Bonhoeffer: Reminiscences by His Friends.* New York: Harper and Row, 1966.

INDEX